CHALLENGING WALKS
WALKS
North-West England
& North Wales

Ron Astley

Copyright ©, R. A. Astley, 1994

Published by Sigma Leisure – an imprint of
Sigma Press, 1 South Oak Lane, Wilmslow, Cheshire SK9 6AR, England.

British Library Cataloguing in Publication Data
A CIP record for this book is available from the British Library.

ISBN: 1-85058-375-7

Typesetting and Design: Sigma Press, Wilmslow, Cheshire.

Maps: designed by the author and produced by Orbit Design.

Cover photographs: main picture – from the summit of Snowdon towards Y Lliwedd *(Graham Beech)*; inset picture – exploring the Peak District *(Chris Rushton)*.

Cover design: *The Agency*, Wilmslow.

Photographs: by the author except where indicated.

IMPORTANT NOTE TO WALKERS

The information in this guide is given in good faith, and is believed to be accurate at the time of publication. The author and publishers cannot accept responsibility for any problems which may arise as a result of your following the routes. Neither can they accept responsibility for your safety. Some of the routes require mountaincraft as well as walking experience and fitness. **Only you can judge your own competence.**

Contents

INTRODUCTION

THE WALKS

APPENDICES

How Big a Challenge?

One person's challenge is another's Sunday morning stroll. So I'd better start by defining my idea of a challenging walk.

The routes in this guide are twenty to forty miles in length, with a couple of exceptions which have rather a lot of ascent. The majority are in hill or mountain areas. The word 'walk' is used as a convenience. All of the routes offer opportunities for demanding fell or trail running, if that's your fancy.

Long distance walking for fun is not a new phenomenon, of course. Manchester ramblers pioneered the classic Marsden-Edale walk back in the early years of the century. Thomas Firbank popularised the Welsh 3000s almost sixty years ago in his book 'I Bought a Mountain', which seems to have been the 'Year in Provence' of its time.

Today, the devising of long, named walks threatens to become a pastime in itself. The Long Distance Paths Advisory Service has almost five hundred routes on its register, and there must be many more with less official status. There has been a boom in guide book publishing too, but as far as I am aware none since 'The Big Walks' has been devoted to demanding single-day walks. And that twenty-year-old guide concentrated on Scotland, rather than areas closer to home for most of us. I hope that my own book fills part of the gap.

Aims

The task I set myself was to create a score of challenging walks which could be accomplished within a day. The routes should take a natural line. They should preferably be circular. They should be within day or weekend reach of the many walkers living in the North West and West Midlands. And they should be original, in whole or in part.

My aim to make all the routes circular stemmed from an irritation with guides which dump you a long way from home at the end of the day. In some cases, devising return routes has brought its own rewards, by taking me through countryside I would otherwise have regarded as not worthy of a visit.

The last criterion, of originality, proved to be the most difficult to meet, as all the obvious lines are well-explored and repeatedly described. But being able to think in terms of thirty miles or so opened up new possibilities.

I am sure that even the most dedicated long distance walkers will discover many fresh ideas in the guide. Certainly they will find variety. The walks are not confined to mountain areas, and indeed I hope I have been able to demonstrate that challenging walks can be enjoyed very close to home.

Format

I intend the guide to be used both for advance planning and as an active companion in the field. You will see that I have separated out the basic directions from the running commentary and background information by placing it in a parallel column. It would be interesting to have your comments on this style of description.

In view of the length of the walks, it is not practical to give a stile-by-stile description on the few lowland sections. I have assumed that all the people using the guide will be experienced walkers who don't need to be told where to place their feet for every step of the way, so I have given detailed guidance only where routes are not clear.

The large maps will enable you to identify instantly the nature of the route, and to relate it to your maps. It would have been preferable to have all the maps with the same orientation, but this would have meant reducing the 'upright' routes to half size, so we chose the lesser of the evils. Perhaps I am being optimistic, but I think that in many cases it will be possible to guide yourself purely from the map and description.

The distances given are round figures based on map measurements. To suit everybody, I have used 'miles' in the narrative and 'kilometres' in the detail column. Times include an allowance for food-stops. You can treat the times just as an indication, or use them as challenge times. In this case, you should bear in mind that they are usually more demanding than those allowed in challenge walk events. But they are entirely realistic, being generally about ten to fifteen per cent slower than my times. You will have to keep moving briskly, though. If you are a fell runner or trail runner you should comfortably beat the times.

Where they exist, I have shown shorter versions and variants so that parties of two strengths can enjoy the route together, or slower walkers split it into two separate days. Many of the routes start close to youth hostels, so they could be adopted by wardens as local challenge walks.

It seems to have become the custom to give names to walks, so I have joined in the fun and often, regrettably, succumbed to the temptation to invent alliterative titles.

Approach

Before writing this section, I re-read the introductions to several walking guides, and realised anew that they are full of pious exhortations and personal prejudices. Piety is not my style, but I am not going to miss the opportunity to propound my own prejudices.

If you are already an experienced long distance walker, you should probably skip this part. I wouldn't dream of giving you any advice. But if you are just starting to consider longer walks, you might find something of interest in my approach. I should warn you, though, that some people would consider it heretical.

I have lost count of the times I have overtaken people slogging up hills, armoured in big jackets, floppy breeches, knee-length gaiters, long stockings, heavy boots, under the misapprehension they are being sensible. They can never carry enough food to replace the energy they are losing, in the form of heat, as their bodies try to keep cool enough to function efficiently. Adopt this approach for a day of thirty-odd miles on the hills, and you're likely to get very tired and to finish late – if you finish the route at all. There is another way.

I suggest that the most important assurances of safety on long walks are whole-body fitness, with its concomitants of speed and endurance; and equipment that is appropriate for the athletic nature of the activity.

If you feel disagreement welling up inside you, turn quickly to the walks. I don't want to spoil your enjoyment. If you are open minded, stay with me and we'll start by looking at equipment.

Equipment

Let's set the parameters. High performance coupled with low weight, low bulk and minimum restriction to movement are the essential qualities. Usage is in restricted circumstances – you won't be tackling these long routes in the depths of winter because there aren't sufficient hours of daylight. Presumably you are going to have the sense to pick a period of settled weather. So what do you genuinely need to wear and to carry?

I suspect that I am the first person to write a walks guide book who doesn't own any walking boots. Do I hear some squeaks about grip and ankle support? The Walsh fell running shoes I normally wear have a better grip than most heavy rubber soled boots, and don't twist on my feet like ordinary trainers. They are also environmentally friendly, as they don't have sharp edges to erode hillsides. Of course they aren't waterproof. But they dry out on your feet as quickly as they get wet. And anyway, what's so awful about getting your feet wet? Skin is waterproof and can be dried in seconds. It's those 'protective' boots which take days to dry.

Socks are a casualty though. Those dinky white anklets which look so smart on the road or in the gym quickly become disgustingly stained and stiff underfoot. I have only recently discovered an answer: thermal liner socks in Meraklon and Lycra, made by Bridgedale. On the over-elaborate pack (which must account for a third of the price) it states that the socks "ensure dryness and insulation by wicking away moisture from foot to the surface of the sock, where it evaporates". I don't think the manufacturers envisaged a situation where water is squeezing up between the toes. But at least the socks stay warm when wet, and don't dry out hard.

As to support, I have this quaint notion that ankles are jointed to enable feet to adapt to irregularities of surface, so that the body can stay upright, and in balance. Feet have a flex to help forward propulsion. Silly ideas, I know. I'm sure we would all be better off if our ankles and feet were locked in a rigid position – for ice climbing anyway.

So that's one very strong prejudice of mine, in favour of the lightest available footwear. I usually wear Walsh Raids or PB myself, and these are tough enough to survive two or three years of frequent immersions in bogs and subsequent scrubbings in clean water. But a new company, ETA Adventure, has recently introduced a range of ultra-lightweight footwear that appears to be more advanced both in design and materials. Their Challenger shoes are probably most suitable for people who run a substantial part of a route. Wayfarer and Pathfinder shoes have a slightly thicker sole that gives cushioning on hard forest tracks. The Trekker low-cuff boot would be ideal for those who want to enjoy the benefits of ultra light footwear but are doubtful about using shoes on the hills. All these models have a newly-developed sole unit, in an adhesive rubber compound with multi-directional grip, that should perform well on both soft and rocky terrain.

For clothing, the layering principle is widely accepted. I have scanned current ranges to discover if there are any items which meet the criteria particularly well.

I always wear running shorts, because I have them anyway, and because they have minimum bulk when you pull on the next layer. The fabric name to look for is Pertex, a microfibre that is very light and wind-proof. Ronhill Breezemax shorts have the extra benefit of an inner of Coolmax, yet another new miracle fibre. If you prefer less brief shorts, look also for fabrics such as Supplex and Tactel.

For active wear over running shorts, it has to be the stretch leggings universally known as Tracksters, much to the annoyance of the holders of the brand name, Ronhill Sports. It's one of the signs – and penalties – of success when your product name becomes the generic word, like Hoover being used for vacuum cleaners. You can wear genuine Tracksters all year round now, as there are three thicknesses available.

Several manufacturers offer next-to-the-skin layers for the upper body, but all the garments are in fabrics suitable for cool or cold weather. Examples are the Ronhill Fellshirt and the Karrimor ABL shirt, both in Polartec 100.

No company in this country makes a fell shirt designed to cope with the needs of fast movement in warm weather. I have a couple of old Rohan tops in Dunova with a low collar, button neck, button cuffs, which are disintegrating from constant use. If you are in France, take the opportunity to buy a Carline Sun shirt, in Dunova with short sleeves, reinforcement patches on the shoulders for rucksack straps, and a big patch pocket. Meanwhile, British manufacturers are still unable to offer us an alternative to a cotton T-shirt.

Most of us pull on a fleece top for the warmth layer. This is where I made my best discovery. Ultrafleece has been around a long time in Mountain Equipment ranges, and I had assumed it had been outdated by the latest Polartec fabrics. In fact, it meets our criteria of low bulk and low weight much more closely. The latest Ultrafleece tops from ME also have underarm ventilation panels and an extra little front pocket that is perfect for the pencil and paper that guide book writers have to carry. It has become my most-used fleece.

I have always been a little doubtful about shelled fleece because of the possible loss of versatility, but another Mountain Equipment top, the Yukon, uses lightweight Polartec 100, and I found it gave just the right balance of warmth and ventilation for all day wear in changeable spring and autumn weather.

Now we come to the garments that enable you to dramatically reduce the load in your rucksack – lightweight shells. I have a Karrimor Climaguard jacket that has been with me on every hill walk and run for three years. Even just on top of the base layer, it adds considerable warmth and protection. On top of a fleece, it creates an outfit for the winter or the alps. Unfortunately, this model is no longer available, but Karrimor assure me that the replacement Alpiniste shell jacket offers comparable performance. The fabric has a slightly softer feel, and the jacket is longer.

These microfibre shells shrug off showers surprisingly well, but there are versions such as the Karrimor Vector which have rainproof treatments. Shorter in length, the Ronhill Aquabloc top is more suitable for running. There are trousers to match the Alpiniste jacket and, at a lower price, featherlight Breeze trousers from Ronhill.

As for a rucksack, the superlight Karrimor KIMM is *de rigeur* for fell runners, and desirable to everyone else dedicated to fast movement on the hills. I particularly like the lower part of the harness, which has a wide, comfortable belt that carries the load, rather than just acts as a restraining strap. Small exterior zipped pockets are ideal for items such as car keys.

Fuel

If you have accepted the idea of a dynamic approach, apply it to food and drink too. For instance, protein doesn't get absorbed by the body during intensive exercise, so there's not much point in carrying cheese sandwiches. Mashed bananas on granary bread would give you more energy. Copy marathon runners and go in for carbo loading during the previous week, by eating lots of pasta.

It's difficult to carry enough fluid to replace the amount lost in a long day of running or walking. My experience is that isotonic drinks do help to keep the body functioning efficiently, as they replenish mineral salt levels. The cost per litre, made up, is the same as fruit juice. Carbohydrate drinks are the quickest way to give a boost to energy at the end of the day. Isostar and Leppin are the brand names of typical energy drinks.

Fitness

If you go out walking every weekend, your legs at least will attain a degree of fitness. But muscles start to atrophy after two or three days. And walking is not aerobic. Go on, try a little test now. Check your resting pulse rate. Lower than sixty per minute is it?

I suggest that if you seriously want to enhance your ability to walk or run long distances, whole-body fitness training is essential. If you are only just beginning to extend your distance range, work in the gym could help you to make the breakthrough. Most important of all, it will give you an excuse to wear shiny black Lycra shorts.

You could be surprised at the difference weight training, aerobics and circuit training would make to your capabilities. For instance, pyramiding a series of sprints – that is, building up and down in number – does wonders for your recovery times. So you are able to pick up speed immediately you crest a steep rise. Step aerobics gets close to replicating hill climbing if you use a high platform.

Extending the operating range of your body in this way increases your reserves of strength. If you are considering doing some of the longer routes in this guide – especially as I did them, alone – you need the safety margin that a high level of fitness gives you. And anyway, it's fun to be fit.

Pace

Now here's another controversial subject. Let me start by mentioning my own experience. I find that many long distance walkers' pace is too fast for me. It's forced and uncomfortable, out of accord with my breathing. My natural walking pace is about half a mile an hour slower, and my next gear up is a relaxed lope at about ten minute mile pace. On a long route, I alternate between walking and running, depending on the terrain, and I find this to be the least tiring method. It also enables me to look at my surroundings.

The constant-pace people seem to have their bodies tensed, and their breathing tells me they are pressing too hard uphill. (Sorry lads, I've been spying on you). Try both approaches and see which one suits you best.

Challenge Walks

In the last few years, a sport-within-a-sport has developed, of challenge walking. There are about a couple of hundred organised events every year, over distances up to a hundred miles. These walks are controlled by check points, and usually supported with drink or food. Certificates or badges are often available to finishers. Most of the events are organised by the Long Distance Walkers Association. A list of the main events in the area covered by this guide is given after the routes. If you are new to long distance walking, you might prefer to build your confidence by entering a few events.

Enjoy the walks!

VALE ROYAL ROUND

The heart of Cheshire

36mls/57km   12 hrs

Negligible ascent

This first route is not typical of the others in the guide. But it does demonstrate that it is not always necessary to travel to hilly areas to find challenging and satisfying long walks. The Vale Royal Round passes within a mile of my home. I established the basic framework of the route on a fine January Sunday, when I was without a car.

The complete circuit takes you through a surprising variety of river and forest scenery in central Cheshire. You follow natural unobstructed lines rather than stumble from field to field over a multitude of stiles, as is so often the case with lowland paths. Perhaps more than any other route in the guide, it lends itself to different approaches. As a straightforward challenge walk. As a long but easy trail run. Even – dare I suggest it in a guide to challenging walks – as a series of easy trail walks to make up the whole circuit in two or three days. Whichever approach you choose, I am not going to let you go around in ignorance of the many features of interest, even though it makes the description longer than the rest.

OS Landranger Maps 117 & 118

*Vale Royal Tourism Department
The Drumber
Winsford
Cheshire
CW7 1AH
0606 862862*

You can join the circuit at any point, but most people will find Northwich convenient. It's a town founded on salt. Literally. Unrestrained pumping of brine from beneath the town in former centuries often caused dramatic subsidence.

Northwich has lots of pubs, cafés, hotels and free parking

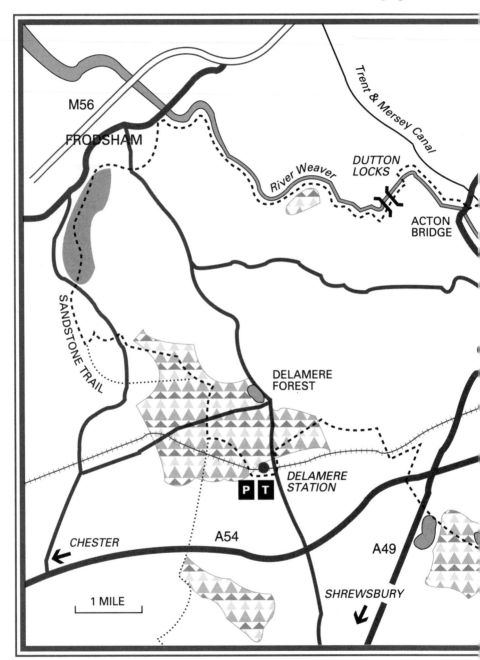

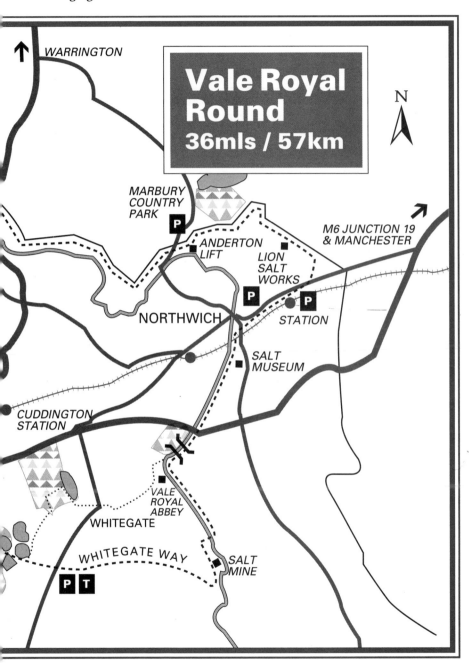

WARRINGTON

Vale Royal Round
36mls / 57km

N

MARBURY COUNTRY PARK

P

ANDERTON LIFT

M6 JUNCTION 19 & MANCHESTER

LION SALT WORKS

P

P

NORTHWICH

STATION

SALT MUSEUM

CUDDINGTON STATION

VALE ROYAL ABBEY

WHITEGATE

WHITEGATE WAY

SALT MINE

P **T**

Buildings were constructed with timber frames to
keep them in one piece, leaving a legacy today of
attractive black and white elevations – Victorian
not Tudor. The salt industry also made the town
into a busy inland port, with its own shipyards on
the River Weaver. Straightening, deepening and
the installation of locks in the eighteenth century
opened up the river to sea-going vessels of up to
1000 tons. The Northwich Salt Museum tells you   *Salt Museum*
more about the history of the salt industry.   *0606 41331*

Cheshire County Council is considering adopting   *GR 670739*
the Vale Royal Round as a new regional trail. The   *Free parking in town*
officially blessed route through Northwich passes   *and at station*
the railway station so I will start the description at
this easily identifiable point.

We are going anti-clockwise so, with your back to
the station, turn right. Put on your dark glasses,
hurry past Tesco and B & Q, turn left at a tyre   *800m to turn*
centre, and the surroundings soon get more rural.
A muddy lane takes you down to a bridge, and
back left. A stile high on the right opens on to a
field and thence to another track leading to the
Trent & Mersey canal. Go down to the right of the
bridge on to the towpath and turn left.

You stay on the canal towpath all the way to
Acton Bridge. The first landmark is the Lion Salt   *Lion Salt Works*
Works, on your left. These derelict buildings   *Discovery Centre*
housed the only remaining open pan salt produc-   *0606 40555*
tion operation in western Europe as recently as
1986. Basically, brine was boiled in huge sauce-
pans to make the water evaporate. Looking at the
buildings, you may be surprised to learn that
restoration is planned.

The open parkland which you can see across the
canal is Marbury Country Park. Back on this side,

you get your first sight of the River Weaver if you didn't prowl round the town before starting the walk. Stop by a small bridge spanning a narrow side channel. This must be where ley lines cross, or something, because it's a hot spot for happenings.

GR 647753

Immediately next to the canal you can see the top of the Anderton boat lift, an unusual example of Victorian engineering. It was built in 1875 to transfer barges up or down the fifty feet high slope between the canal and the river. The industrial site below you is where ICI was founded, as Brunner & Mond. A little to the right, that indispensable material of today, polythene, was developed in 1933. Back down on the river, but three centuries earlier, Colonel Booth fought – and lost – the last battle of the Civil War.

4km on canal to Anderton

I strongly suggest that groups with more than one car attempting the Round in a day should start at the Anderton lift. By shuttling people the two miles from Northwich town centre you will cut out the most urban stretch of the walk, and also reduce the distance to thirty two miles, which is a little more manageable in the day.

Alternative start
Limited parking
Weekday buses

Keep on along the canal side, under a road, and over the top of Barnton tunnel. I have twice seen parrots here! Descend on tarmac to a wide pool in front of Saltersford tunnel. Beyond, the surroundings are entirely rural, with a wooded bank on the right and the Weaver below you on the left. Turn left at bridge 208 down a path to where a swing bridge carries the A49 across the river. A service road gives easy walking by the water to Dutton locks.

4km from Anderton.
Pub food

Outside the row of cottages there is usually a sign-board giving interesting information on river traffic. Cross over the locks to the western side of the river. In front is the twenty arch span of Dutton viaduct, opened in 1836 for the Grand Junction Railway and still carrying the main west coast railway line. I wonder how many of our new concrete bridges will last this long?

Grassy meadows take you to Pickerings lock – which isn't there now. Opposite the former lock keeper's cottage, you have to turn left along a path, then sharp right through a caravan site. Follow the arrows through a garden gate – I always feel a little guilty even though it is a right of way – and over a stile back on to the riverside.

3km 500m from Acton Bridge

The path now stays close to the river all the way to Frodsham, sometimes through meadows, sometimes through woods which reach down to the waterside. You emerge suddenly on to a busy main road, which you follow to the left for only a few minutes. A signpost 'Bridleway to Overton' directs you up shallow steps, between hedges.

7km to Frodsham

400m on road

Sorry! From its further end you will have to endure townscape for twenty minutes. Continue past houses, cross a main road into Church Lane, turn left into School Lane, then head diagonally left towards an obvious opening into woodland below sandstone cliffs. Take the highest path until you are under the rock and scramble up directly to the war memorial. If you have chosen a clear day for the walk, the view will be extensive, from the cathedrals of Liverpool to the Clwyd Hills.

Food and beds in Frodsham

This is where you join the Sandstone Trail, which links a series of outcrops from here to the Shropshire border. It is identified by a yellow footprint

with the letter S. The Trail squiggles entertain-
ingly along the edge of the escarpment, above
woodland. Where the rock fades away into the
hillside, the Sandstone Trail swings sharply left
over the rim. A few paces to the left on top of the
rise there is an area of short turf I keep mown
especially as a lunch spot for Vale Royal Roun-   *2km from memorial*
ders.

Fed and watered, you will enjoy the stroll down a   *1km 400m to road*
sunken path through birch woods. At a lane, turn
left then almost immediately right over a stile.
The Trail dips in and out of fields and bluebell
woods to a lane with a hinge top stile. You leave   *GR 520732*
the Trail temporarily here, turn left, left again,   *600m on road*
then right up a farm road, Where this track bends
right, go through a field gate directly in front and
follow the hedge round to a stile on to a lane.
Turn right and take the second footpath sign on   *750m on road*
the left into Delamere Forest.

A pleasant path along the edge of woodland takes
you into the heart of the main forest, 2,400 acres
of pines and firs. Just after an isolated cottage,
turn right down a slight hill and up a short rise to
rejoin the Sandstone Trail coming in from the
right. Turn left, cross a road at a car park, and   *Toilets*
continue through lines of beech trees to a forest
track crossroads. You now leave the Sandstone   *Left in 600m*
Trail finally and turn left to Delamere Station.

Now, I realise that you would not normally be   *Food and toilets*
tempted inside the station café for a pot of tea and
homemade pastries and cheesecake. But this is the
critical point of the walk. The crux you could say.
So you might have to put personal feelings aside
for the sake of weaker members of the party.
Delamere Station is also the most convenient
place to get the train back to Northwich for those   *Train to Northwich*

splitting the Round into two sections. The current
timetable offers a train at four thirty, but do
check.

From the café, go up steps to the road, turn left
over the bridge and take the first public track on
the right into the eastern section of forest. Follow   *1km in forest*
as straight a line as possible, and you will emerge
on to a sandy lane which soon joins a narrow
surfaced road. It's no hardship to have tarmac
under your feet to the Forest View Inn cross
roads. Turn right down the hill and left at the   *2km on road*
bottom along a concession path to Whitegate
Way.

This flat, sheltered trail follows the line of a   *Car park, toilets*
former railway for almost six miles through pine   *halfway*
and birch woods, with glimpses of reed fringed
meres through the trees. It's a surprise to find
yourself confronted at the end by industrial buildings. They are the visible part of Britain's only
rock salt mine. Six hundred feet below your feet,
tunnels big enough to take 30 ton trucks stretch
out for six miles under the Cheshire countryside.

Turn left past the salt mine, then right just before   *800m on road*
a narrow bridge and you will find yourself back
by the River Weaver. Cross to the east bank and
head north.

This is my favourite part of the Weaver Valley.
It's particularly delightful in early summer. Irises
crowd in upon the path, bluebells carpet the
wooded banks, herons flap lazily across the water.

Beyond the tree tops on the opposite bank you
will catch glimpses of 'the roof of Vale Royal   *Vale Royal Abbey*
Abbey. Or to be more accurate, the house built on
its site. The present building dates back only to

1812, when it was built for Baron Delamere. It is a
rather gloomy and dilapidated sandstone mansion
apparently of no special historical or architectural
interest. But hidden within its walls are the
remains of a Tudor house and medieval monastic
buildings. Alongside under the turf are the foundations of what was once the largest Cistercian
abbey church in England.

The Weaver Valley

If you have wondered about the name Vale Royal,
it originated in the thirteenth century with
Edward I. He put up the cash for the abbey
church. 421 feet in length and 232 feet across the
transepts, it must have been an impressive sight.
Little is known of the abbey history, but it seems
likely that there was a partial collapse during
construction. I think the builders must have been

ancestors of the men who built the extension to my house. After Henry VIII took a hand, the stones were used to build the Tudor mansion.

There is a resident ghost of Ida the nun, who had an illicit affair with one of the monks. I can assure you that it is very spooky round the abbey at night.

Unfortunately, the House has attracted the attention of developers wanting to link its restoration to the building of an estate of fifty houses and a golf course. Which is of greater value to the community – the restoration of an interior or the preservation of a classic piece of English landscape? A ten minute detour across the river at *2km to locks* Vale Royal locks will enable you to make up your own mind.

You're on the home stretch now. In front, the main London railway line crosses the valley on a high viaduct. Through the arches, over riverside meadows, under the busy A556, past a forest of yacht masts in a boatyard, and very suddenly you *4km to town centre* find yourself back in Northwich town centre.

If you want to return to the railway station, follow the path alongside the railway line past a *1km to station* park and a cemetery. If your car is in one of the central car parks, turn left at the railway bridge and right at the traffic lights.

I hope you enjoy your day discovering the landscape and history of Vale Royal.

Delamere Forest

Short Circuits

The easiest way to split the route into two sections is to make use of the train service between
Delamere or Cuddington station, and Northwich
station, on the Chester to Manchester line.

There are two footpath links which enable you to
split the route into three sections. The northern
link is an unimaginative sequence of paths from   *Delamere Way*
Acton Bridge to Delamere. By contrast, the south-
ern link makes up one of the best modest length
walks in mid-Cheshire.

At Vale Royal locks, cross the river, go in front of   *Start from Northwich*
the Abbey, down the beech avenue to Whitegate.   *or the Whitegatre*
(It is here that the housing estate will be built). A   *Way Car park*
path on the northern side of the church signed
'Dalefords Lane' leads past a pool, along a board
walk section, round the back of a half-timbered
house to Pettypool. Follow the trail up through
the woods, cross over the lane, and a sign points   *10miles/16km circuit*
you across Newchurch Common to the halfway
point on Whitegate Way, where you turn left on
the main route.

Other trail walking opportunities

Cheshire offers other long circuits. For instance,
starting at Beeston Castle, you can go south on
the Sandstone Trail to its junction with the Trent
& Mersey canal, and return to Beeston anti-clockwise. Or, longer, turn west along the Marches
Way to Chester and back to Beeston via the
northern arm of the canal.

TOPS & BOTTOMS

The best of the Western Peak

25mls/40km   9 hrs
Ascent: 3000ft/915m

I'll be honest. The western fringe of the Peak District is not one of my favourite areas. Despite its closeness to home, I rarely walk there. To me, the landscape has an end-of-time feeling, the earth seems to lack vitality, even the rocks are decaying. But then, I always was a sensitive soul.

OS Outdoor Leisure White Peak Map

However, I have put my personal feelings aside and unselfishly muddied my trainers to find the perfect circuit for all you Peak freaks. I was able to link together the high points, both in terms of altitude and interest, and to eliminate road sections almost entirely. On a bright Spring day, I almost enjoyed the walk.

There are four possible starting points with good parking, but the best is Clough House in Wildboarclough, as effort and interest are then spread evenly throughout the day. The valley is one of several places where the last wild boar in England is supposed to have been killed. There's no life wilder than the farmers there now, if you ignore occasional sightings of a black puma.

Start at Clough House GR 988699 Car Park

It's a classic start to a walk. From the lane at the back of the car park, a broad track over sheep-cropped grass takes you to a bridge across a stream, then climbs Cumberland Clough on a shelf above a tree-lined miniature ravine.

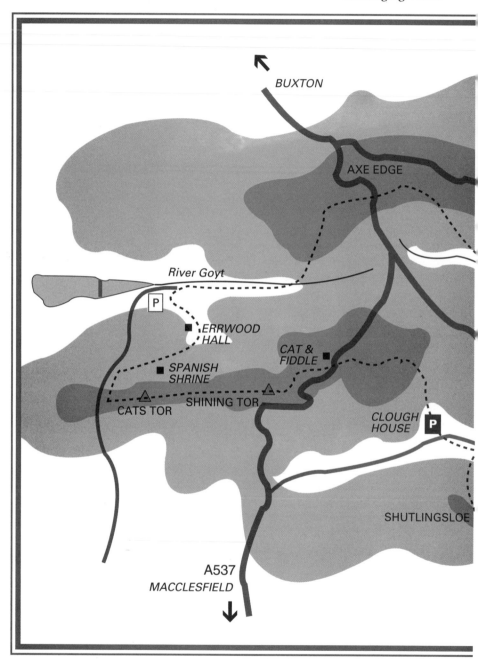

BUXTON

AXE EDGE

River Goyt

P

ERRWOOD
HALL

CAT &
FIDDLE

SPANISH
SHRINE

CATS TOR

SHINING TOR

CLOUGH
HOUSE

P

SHUTLINGSLOE

A537
MACCLESFIELD

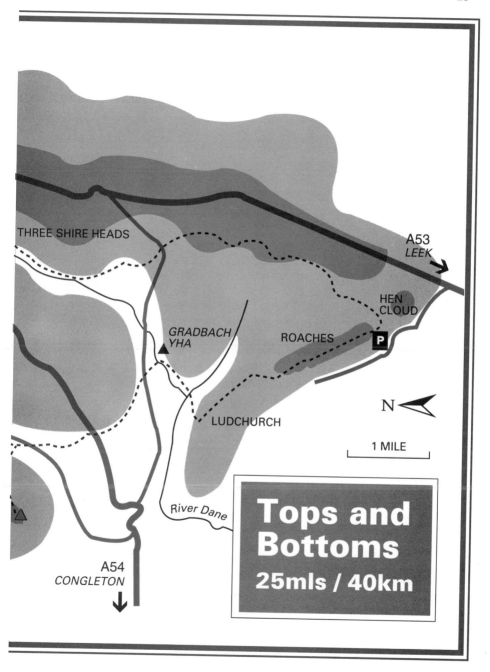

THREE SHIRE HEADS

A53
LEEK

HEN
CLOUD

GRADBACH
YHA

ROACHES

P

LUDCHURCH

N

1 MILE

River Dane

**Tops and
Bottoms**
25mls / 40km

A54
CONGLETON

Almost too soon, you meet the open moorland at   *Left in 1km*
a cross trail. Turn left and mount more steeply to
Danebower Hollow, a well used bridleway con-
necting the Macclesfield and Congleton roads.
Turn left again at a sign post and the Cat and   *Left in 900m*
Fiddle Inn comes into view.

The only theory I can remember for the origin of   *Left at pub*
the name is that it is a corruption of 'Ketner
fidele' – presumably an eighteenth century French
exile proclaiming his loyalty to Louis a safe distance from the guillotine. The present building
dates from 1823 and is of course the second
highest pub in England.

Cross the road at the Cat and Fiddle, turn left,   *Right in 200m*
then keep right through a gate on to what was
probably the original road. Curve round above
the Shining Tor Café – I rather liked its former
name of Dish and Spoon. Beyond a ladder stile,   *Left in 1km*
look for stone steps mounting a wall on the left. A
much-repaired path takes you to Shining Tor, a
notably inappropriate name. You'll have to pop
over a wall to stand on the actual summit.

The way on leads along the top of the broad
ridge. At first, you can keep your footwear clean.
Soon, though, you're hopping from side to side of
a glutinous black trough. If you're wearing leather
boots, you're probably also wearing a smirk. But
it is the procession of hard-edged stiff soles like
yours that caused this erosion in the first place.
Think about it.

Continue over Cats Tor to Pyms Chair and the   *Right in 4km*
narrow road that crosses into the Goyt Valley.
This is the only significant stretch of road in the
circuit. As it's downhill, you'll only be on tarmac
for ten minutes, to a small layby and a signpost   *Right in 900m*
pointing right to Errwood Hall.

You won't find a grand house. It was built in the 1830s by the Grimshawe family, and demolished in the 1930s by the water authority when they created the lower of two reservoirs. Only the foundations remain. The most poignant reminders of the past are three memorials to the dead.

You will see the first as you descend into the wooded valley. Sequestered in the first group of trees is a small round building, like a dovecote with a cross on top. It's the Spanish shrine, commemorating a treasured governess of the family who died in 1889.

Shrine to the governess of the Grimshawe family (photo: Graham Beech)

Follow the path down to the stream, cross over   *Yellow arrows*
the wooden bridge then turn back sharp left to
the top of a knoll. On top is the private burial
ground of the Grimshawe family. One stone
records the death of a Bayonne-born girl at only
27. This cloudy valley must have seemed a long
way from the sun of southern France. Another
grave is of Captain Butler, who commanded the
Grimshawe private yacht. The early death of the
servants seems more sad to me than the passing
of their 'masters'.

Retrace your steps to the wide path which passes
round the western side of the knoll. The hall
remains are up on the left. When you see the car   *2km from road to car*
park wall, follow the trail around to the right,   *park*
above the valley lane. Cross over to a green shelf
through the woods above the River Goyt. You
coincide with the road again at a packhorse
bridge moved from lower down the valley.
Scramble up the bank to the road, and walk along
to the signpost pointing left to Old Buxton across
a wooden bridge. Or cross the stone bridge and   *Left in 2km*
follow a muddy trod to the same place.

It's a pleasant stroll alongside the stream up Berry
Clough, particularly on a bright Autumn day
when the heather is in bloom. The track crosses
the stream, then divides when it gains open moor-
land. Go right, cross the old coach road, then the   *Fork right in 1km*
new Buxton road. As you draw level with the Axe
Edge skyline, keep right at a fork to meet the lane
that nips across from the Leek road to the Congle-
ton road. Turn right and almost immediately left   *2km 500m*
at a Three Shire Heads sign.

Over a stile, the Dane Valley opens up in front of
you. A green trail drops down to join a tarmac
farm road. Continue down the side of the stream,

through a gate and back on to a sandy track.
Suddenly, you find yourself at a stone packhorse
bridge over the young River Dane.

2km 500m from road

This is Three Shire Heads, where Staffordshire,
Cheshire and Derbyshire meet. Legend has it that
criminals fleeing from the police were able to
escape capture by stepping across the boundaries.
I doubt it. But certainly this bridge was much
used by packhorse traders carrying salt from
Cheshire. A broadening of the stream still carries
the name of Panniers Pool.

You can't complain that I don't find you some
especially pleasant spots for lunch. Lunch? Yes,
you're only half way round, but you're nearer the
end of this description because there's less for me
to witter on about from now on. So lean back on
the grass in this sheltered hollow and enjoy your
sandwiches.

Your lunch will digest quietly as you stroll on
down by the river. The path joins a farm road   *Left in 900m*
which swings left out of the valley then curves
round a low hillside. At the top of the rise, a
green track forks off right, drops to a metal bridge
over a stream, then climbs steeply to Spring Head.   *Fork right*
The right of way goes up steps on the left-hand
side of the cottage facing you, then contours
round to another lane and Flash Bottom.

Resist the temptation to obey and just bear right
behind the buildings, cross a rivulet and head up   *Turn right*
the slope by a wall. Follow a trod round a small
pocket of moorland and through a gap in the
wall, passing to the right of a farm. An indistinct
path over rough pasture takes you on to a farm
track and to a T-junction above Gib Hill.

Cumberland Clough

Follow the lane opposite down a short hill and take the second opening on the right through the trees. A stile over a new wire fence admits you to a nature reserve. You walk along a shallow valley between two lines of rocks and emerge at another T-junction. Go straight on again, fork right and turn left down a farm road. This runs into a sunken trail which takes you on to the saddle between the Roaches and Hen Cloud.

Right in 200m

400m on lane

The name of this long outcrop probably originates in the French 'roches'. It's very popular with north west climbers because the rock is sharper-edged than the sandstone edges of Stanage, Frog-gat and Curbar above the Derwent. Brightly clothed figures are usually gesticulating on top of the cliff. If you want to see climbers in action, walk along the foot of the first section.

For the purposes of this route description, how-ever, you saunter along the top of the Roches, enjoying the views and the change of terrain from moorland path to rocky trail. You've done most of the hard work now. Drop off the northern end of the ridge at Roche End, slide through a narrow gap in the wall, and descend a bouldery path into woodland. A signpost directs you left to Lud Church.

Lud Church is a deep cleft in the rock used as a secret meeting place by Lollards, medieval religi-ous dissenters. Its mystery has been dissipated by an over-abundance of signposting. The path you are on leads you down steps into the one-time dead end of the cleft and delivers you on to a broad path, facing a castle-like rock outcrop.

2km from Roche End

Turn right and descent to Gradbach Youth Hostel by the River Dane. The hostel is an ideal over-

night base for the route. There is an obvious
connection from here to Three Shire Heads for
those wanting to spread the walk over two days.

Did you think all the climbing was over? Cross   *Left at hostel*
the metal bridge over the river and your legs face
almost their last test up a boulder-strewn slope.
From the road at Burntcliff Top a path rises just
high enough to give you a view of Shutlingsloe.
People with a great deal of imagination have
called this hill the Matterhorn of the Peak District.

Cross the A54 at stiles into a field. Keep a barn on   *1km 600m road to*
your right, go over another stile in a wall and   *road*
head for a gap in the trees that fringe Wildboarclough. Keep these on your right as you descend
into the valley until you see where an arrow on a
post directs you diagonally down towards the
Crag Inn. A gap in the stone walls at the corner of   *1km to inn*
the field gives access to a narrow path and a
bridge almost directly opposite the pub.

I mention the building only as a guide to naviga-   *Turn right*
tion. I appreciate that you would not want to be
diverted so close to the end of the walk. Turn
right and immediately left up a surfaced track   *First left*
leading to Shutlingsloe. Despite its striking lack of
similarity to a Swiss peak, the hill is still better
looked at than from, as the view from the top to
the west reminds you of the closeness of urban
sprawl. But if you've never been up you may as   *1km to top*
well grab the opportunity. Me, I'm forking right
through the Bank Top Farm gate and following
the shelf trail above the wood. A quarter of an
hour will see me clambering over the high ladder
stile on to the road, in sight of the car park. See   *1km 100m to car*
you back at the Crag Inn.   *park.*

DERWENTDALE WATERSHED

A bog trotter's delight

28 miles/45km   10 hours
Ascent: 2,300ft/700m

The Derwent Watershed is one of the most fam- *OS Outdoor Leisure*
ous long walks in the Peak District. I have always *Map Dark Peak*
seen it as an amalgam of two rather better walks,
each with its own appeal. Judge for yourself by
trying them both.

The first route follows what might be called the *Start at GR 203859*
true Derwent watershed, the circle of high moors *Heatherdene car park*
around the Derwent reservoir. It gives you a rich
helping of Bleaklow's bogs, the chance to get
away from crowded paths, and a memorable finish along gritstone edges, straight down to a pub.
What more could you ask for?

Answering my own question, how about a car
park posh enough to have a name. And it's free.
Thank you Forestry Commission. The car park is
just off the road between Yorkshire Bridge and
the T junction. So you'll start the walk with a *1 km on road*
stroll across the two long Ladybower bridges.

The footpath goes off on the left just inside the
road to Derwent reservoir. Head up the field
through a gate then follow the green NT arrows
as they shunt you round Crookhill Farm. You end
up on a bridle path. Go to the right then bear left
over the rise. You start to get double views now,
of Kinder Scout on the left and reservoirs and
forests on the right.

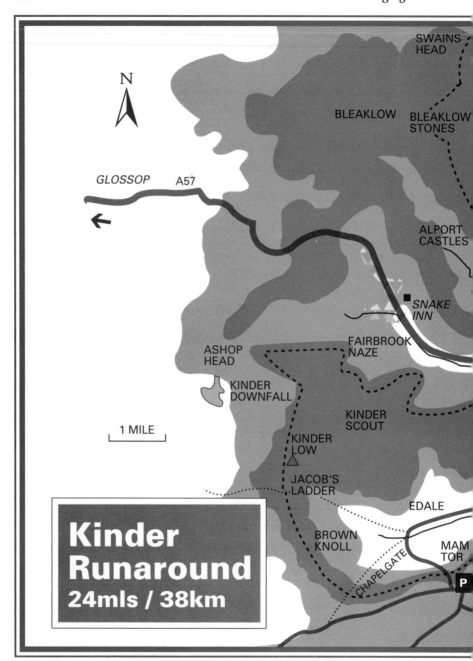

N

GLOSSOP   A57

SWAINS
HEAD

BLEAKLOW   BLEAKLOW
STONES

ALPORT
CASTLES

SNAKE
INN

ASHOP
HEAD

FAIRBROOK
NAZE

KINDER
DOWNFALL

1 MILE

KINDER
SCOUT

KINDER
LOW

JACOB'S
LADDER

EDALE

BROWN
KNOLL

MAM
TOR

CHAPELGATE

P

**Kinder
Runaround**
24mls / 38km

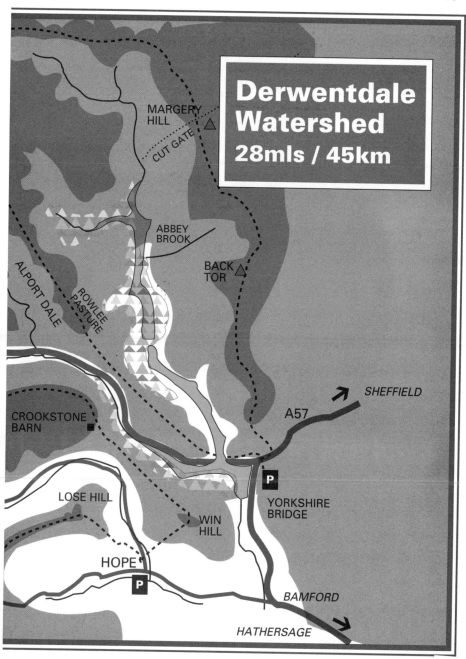

MARGERY HILL

CUT GATE

Derwentdale Watershed 28mls / 45km

ABBEY BROOK

BACK TOR

ALPORT DALE

ROWLEE PASTURE

SHEFFIELD

A57

CROOKSTONE BARN

P

YORKSHIRE BRIDGE

LOSE HILL

WIN HILL

HOPE

P

BAMFORD

HATHERSAGE

The path is well signposted, and takes you across   *4km from farm*
another bridleway to the boundary of open coun-
try. A wide green trail mounts over Rowlee Pasture and skirts behind the rock pinnacles of
Alport Castles. There's an exhilarating feeling of
space, being poised between two valleys.

Keep an eye open to the left. When you are
opposite the northern end of two fir plantations in
the Alport valley you must go straight on rather
than follow the rim path to the left. It's wide open
walking again up here, over increasingly wet   *10km GR 115963*
ground. Soon you're climbing a low ridge and
puzzling your way through a maze of gullies to
Bleaklow Stones.

The most obvious path from the Stones heads   *North east for 1km*
down gently on the right. This will take you to   *then north*
the reservoir. Instead, keep to the top of the flat
ridge on a roughly north east bearing. Now, can
you see another small outcrop in front? Yes? Then
you've probably come too far. You should have
turned north a little way back. But all is not lost.
Just about where you are, a wide sandy floored
grough slopes down to the left. Follow it and
you'll find thin trods going left again around the
top of a very shallow valley to Swains Head.

There's a satisfying feeling of isolation on this
long semicircle round the far reaches of the Derwent valley, only a little softened by distant views
of Yorkshire industry. The accepted route is to
follow the stakes marking a local authority
boundary, but with all the detours necessary to
avoid the deepest bogs, it's easy to lose sight of
them.

A flat, green splashy section offers temporary
relief. Keep to the watershed – don't be tempted

out to the Horse Stones on the edge of the hill. As you swing more south, the ground underfoot gradually improves. Your arrival at Cut Gate seems long overdue, but its sudden appearance is still a surprise. Last time I went round the route, I was forewarned by the sight of a purple shape moving with mysterious smoothness across my line of vision. It proved to be a mountain biker using this old trackway across the moors.

10km to Cut Gate
GR 185961

Derwentdale

You could be forgiven for thinking there's just a pleasant stroll now along a series of gritstone outcrops. But if you are tempted to follow the western rim path too far, you will find yourself being taken down the flank of Abbey Brook to the reservoirs.

Walking back by the water edge is an alternative that has a lot to recommend it. If you descend too low, it is certainly better than trying to fight your way across the deep clough of Abbey Brook, with its trackless heather and tussocks too tall to see over. But it's better still to keep high from Margery Hill and curve a little east to Back Tor.

The hard work really is over when you reach here. The path becomes increasingly well used as you tick off the outcrops – Cakes and Bread, Salt Cellar, Wheel Stones. Indeed, large stone slabs have been laid in one section to take the wear from many feet.

Keep high right to the tip of the ridge. At last, you can see Ladybower reservoir and the car park below you. The path brings you out just behind the Ladybower Inn, only a few minutes from your car.

You will probably be well within the ten hours I have allowed, but I thought I would be generous in case you had problems up in the bogs or round Abbey Brook.

KINDER RUNAROUND

Lose to win the long way

24mls/38km   8 hrs

Ascent: 2,750ft/840m

The circuit of the Kinder Scout edges from Edale is a deservedly popular walk of around fifteen miles. The least satisfying section is the southern half, not least because it involves joining the herds of people trudging up Grindsbrook. The ridge on the other side of the valley offers a more defined line, and is of course the first part of the 40 mile Derwent Watershed walk.

OS Outdoor Leisure Map Dark Peak

FOR SKETCH MAP, see previous walk!

Merge the two routes and you have a high level circuit that is one of the most suitable in the guide for running. Once you have gained height you keep it until the last few minutes, and most of the ground underfoot is firm. So let's see how much we can cut off the eight hour walking time.

A hard surface start from Hope village down the Edale road gives your breathing a chance to adapt to a fast rhythm. I can never pass the Cheshire Cheese Inn without remembering the evening I spent there playing darts with a very challenging young woman. Do you ever wonder what your reaction would be if you met an old love? Would the spark still glow? I'm going to risk dedicating this walk to my erstwhile darts partner. Anonymously.

Start at Hope GR 172835 Pay-and-display carpark. Railway station.

I hope you're not letting your thoughts stray, too. The hardest ascent is just in front. After the pub,

Left in 1km 200m

fork left up a lane, then take the first left to the
start of a path on the right. Lose Hill is steadily
steep from this side so there's no point in pushing
too hard. I've never known whether the correct
pronunciation rhymes with booze or with dose.
Perhaps someone can also tell me who coined the
grandiose name of Great Ridge for the broken hill
crests continuing to the west of Lose Hill.

Left in 300m

A brisk walk will suffice along here. Enjoy being
poised between Edale and the Hope valley and
admire the artistic smoke trails from the cement
works chimney. Mam Tor will be busy with
people preparing to throw themselves off the cliff
attached to flimsy frameworks of nylon. You
would think they could find themselves something more sensible to do, like running twenty
four miles round Kinder Scout.

4km from Lose Hill

Across the road, Rushup Edge gives you your
first chance to stretch out your legs and trot past
the boot-laden walkers. Bear right at the wall to
cut across to Chapel Gate. The wide trough in
front slowly steepens to give you an early test of
fitness. Brown Knoll levels out again and drops to
Edale Cross above Jacobs Ladder.

Diagonal right at
GR 103831

6km

The erosion of the hillside in front has been so
severe that large steps have been engineered. It's
back to a walk again. Just about here, a couple of
years ago, I converged with three female fell
runners with one male -greedy so-and-so. One of
the girls commented to me: "There must be a
moral in this somewhere". As always in these
chance encounters, I was unable to make a
memorable response. Even a couple of hours later,
I hadn't thought of anything more profound than
"Don't wear white socks". I don't think that
would have made her rush to write her telephone
number on my shorts do you?

Where the track levels out and curves round to the right you have to find your own way straight on, to come out on the eastern edge of Kinder. Kinder Low top is on your right. The going gets firmer now, on that coarse sand which is so typical of the plateau. Provided you can place your feet adroitly among the stones you can run all the way to the Downfall. There's a sort of miniature estuary here which usually offers shelter whichever way the wind is blowing. But you weren't thinking of stopping for more than a drink were you?

3km from Edale Cross

Follow the line of the Pennine Way along the rim to the north west corner of Kinder. As soon as the

Right in 1km 500m

Kinder Low

path starts to descend towards Ashop Head, turn
sharp right. This northern edge is indistinct at
first, but soon gives you an escarpment to follow.

The eight miles or so to Crookstone Barn must be
one of the finest hill runs in the Peak. The path is
generally level to Fairbrook Naze, but over bouldery terrain that keeps your feet guessing. Cut
across the corner at the nose, to save getting
involved with the rocks. From the stream, heather
starts to take over. The gentle downgrade under
Madwoman's Stones encourages you to break into   *12km to savour*
a glorious gallop, the fastest section of the day.

At Crookstone Barn you have to sidestep left to   *Fork left in 500m*
the old Roman road. Don't go speeding down the
track too far. The day has to finish on top of Win
Hill, the twin of Lose Hill. So keep high, along-
side the wood, until you can cut up to the sum-   *5km from Crookstone*
mit. I like to relax here, finish off any drink that is
left, and look back at Kinder. If you're still with
me, it will be about five hours since we left Hope.   *2km*
Another twenty minutes will see you back at your
car.

Of course, you can always walk round instead.

WEST OF WENLOCK

A stroll in central Shropshire

25mls/40km 9 hrs

Ascent: 1,800ft/550m

On the map, Wenlock Edge makes a long diagonal stripe of contour lines. The end-to-end traverse is an obvious walk, but unfortunately it doesn't work out so well on the ground. For much of the distance, the path is buried in trees, offering little variety and only limited views. For the guide, I did complete the traverse, and then tried to link back to my start near Much Wenlock along field paths on the southern side of the Edge. After wading through knee high corn and being molested by herds of cows, I gave up and ran back along the road in a thunder storm. If you check it out on the map, you'll realise the whole circuit is rather a long way, too.

I turned my attention westwards, to those delectable hills facing the Long Mynd – Caer Caradoc and The Lawley. As you drive down the A49 from Shrewsbury, their skyline shapes are so seductive, you want to stroke them. Because their traverse takes up only half a day, long distance walkers tend to neglect them. But linked up with the central part of Wenlock Edge, the most open section, they help to create a very worthwhile circuit within the capabilities of most walkers, and suitable for all times of the year.

You couldn't find a pleasanter starting point than Church Stretton, nestling at the foot of the Long

OS Landranger Map 137

Tourist Centre 0694 723133

Start at Church Stretton GR 454936

Mynd. A hundred years ago it was a favourite Victorian spa town, an alternative retirement home to Malvern for elderly Indian army officers. Fortunately for us, its popularity faded in the twentieth century so its charming centre has survived relatively unharmed by out-of-character development.

Car park Railway station

The Lawley

Walk down the main shopping street past the station, across the A49 and turn immediately left along Watling Street North. Follow this lane to where it turns sharp right into a housing estate and take the narrow surfaced lane which goes almost straight on. At the end of the tarmac a sign states, unnecessarily, that the continuation up a stony stream bed between high banks is 'Unsuitable for motors'. I'll be kind and tell you there's a

Cross A49 Turn left. Straight on at Helmeth Road. Not the track. 1km from centre

footpath alternative hidden on the left, next to the gate to New House Farm.

Cross a field to a gate and stile at the start of a wide trail through woodland, and follow this as it curves up round the eastern shoulder of Caer Caradoc. An obvious scar leads up from a stile directly to a skyline outcrop. The steep climb makes you understand why a hill fort was built on top. There's not much trace left of the old banks and ditches. It's the view that grabs your interest, a three hundred and sixty degree panorama over the border country.

Left at stile 900m from gate. Ippikin's Way sign.

Caer Caradoc 459m

To the north, the grassy spine of The Lawley invites you onwards. Drop down the northern flank of Caradoc over recently ploughed land and cross a stile to a lane. Turn left to join one lane, then another, and take the first track on the right. Where this goes through a gate to skirt the hill, turn right along the fence to a stile and gate at the foot of the wide green trail which runs the length of The Lawley.

Descend to stile.

Left across two junctions. Right in 200m to gate

This is the steepest side of the hill. At the top, you get another chance to enjoy the view, the Long Mynd sprawling away to the west, the Shropshire plain stretching out to the north beyond The Wrekin. There's a strange weather vane, perched on top of a very long pole.

The Lawley 377m

The long north ridge of The Lawley is a delight. It's very much like a miniature version of the Malvern hills. At the bottom, swing right through a few trees to a gate and the road.

2km grassy promenade

It's a very quiet lane which carries little traffic. Follow it up round a bend alongside a wood to the top of a low ridge. An obvious trail goes back

1km 700m on lane.

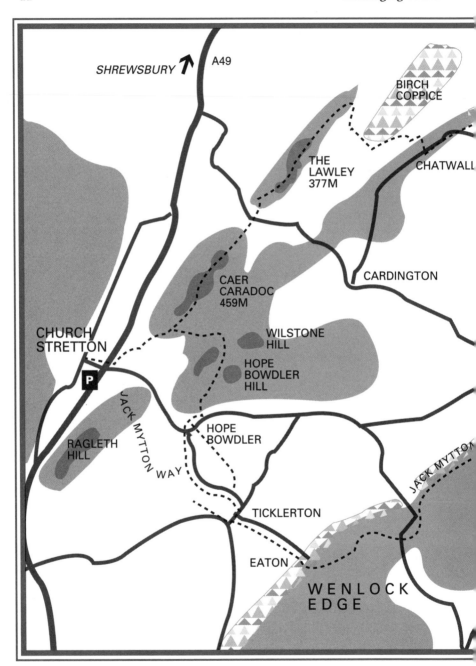

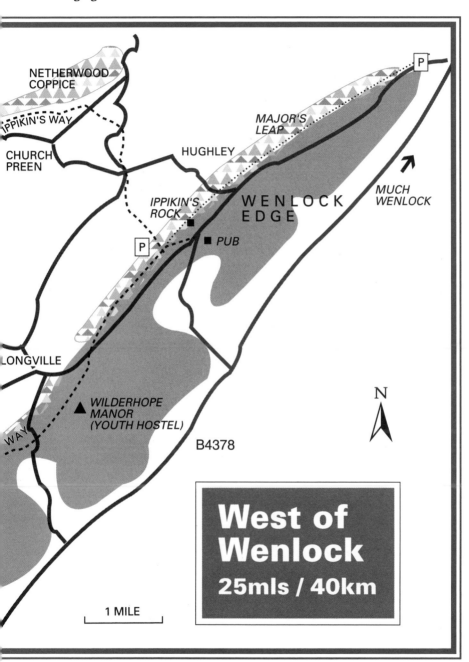

NETHERWOOD
COPPICE

IPPIKIN'S WAY

CHURCH
PREEN

MAJOR'S
LEAP

HUGHLEY

IPPIKIN'S
ROCK

W E N L O C K
E D G E

MUCH
WENLOCK

P

■ PUB

N

LONGVILLE

WAY

▲ WILDERHOPE
MANOR
(YOUTH HOSTEL)

B4378

**West of
Wenlock**

25mls / 40km

1 MILE

at a very sharp angle, on the left, at the back of Birch Coppice. At the end of the trail, clamber over a broken down gate and cross a field to a stile bearing the strange Ippikin's Way sign. Don't bother to try to get a leaflet on this named trail. It was devised for walking holiday companies, and a description is not available to you and me.

Sharp left on path to gate
Straight on to stile

Bear right at the stile to the corner of a group of trees, cross a brook, then turn left along the valley to a gate and a lane. Turn right up the hill, left and left again, to a cottage.

Diagonally right then left to gate. 800m on road

A wide path goes down by the side of the house, but you have to swing right over a field immediately next to the building. At the top corner of the field, cross a stile wearing – yes, you've guessed – the Ippikin's Way sign. Keep along the edge of Netherwood Coppice, over stiles. After two new metal gates a fence swings you away from the trees, across three fields and past a farm to the road.

Left at cottage

2km 800m road to road

Turn right and almost immediately you will see a private drive on the left leading to Preen Manor. Despite the lack of signs, this is a right of way. Follow it for a couple of hundred yards to where a signpost points left. Cross fields to a scruffy farm and a lane.

Turn right.
Fork left.
200m on drive.
Left

Turn right along the lane to a crossroads. Keep straight on to where the road bends right, and take the unsurfaced lane on the left. This deteriorates and disappears entirely after crossing a brook despite indications on the map. Follow a hedge across a field past a house to a gate opening on to a lane head.

Right for 1km on lane. Straight on. Left in 450m.

Keep outside garden

Wenlock Edge is immediately in front of you now. The lane climbs towards the trees, bends right, and passes under a bridge. Turn right on the upper side of the bridge to gain access to the line of a former railway. This is an alternative starting point for people who approach from the West Midlands. Access is from the road running along the top of the escarpment.

Alternative start
GR 564958
Limited parking

Large groups starting from here might like to arrange parking with the friendly landlord of the Wenlock Edge Inn, just above, on the promise of eating there at the end of the day. I called in after my abortive traipse round the southern paths, unfortunately on the day the kitchens were closed, and had to sit facing the menu salivating at the thought of nearly-meals. As this is the halfway point for Stretton starters, the Inn would make an ideal lunch stop too.

Wenlock Edge Inn,
Hilltop 074636 403
Ten minutes via path
off trail north of
bridge

Also close to here is Ippikin's Rock, the origin of the Way name, and supposedly once the haunt of a band of robbers. Dare I suggest they were the first 'ippies? Further towards Much Wenlock, the map indicates Major's Leap, where a military member of the Wilderhope Manor family jumped his horse over a cliff to escape Roundhead pursuers in the civil war. I've always thought the horse should have got the credit – after all, it did all the work and suffered the greatest penalty. A visit to either place is an underwhelming experience.

Tourist attractions

Let's get back to the walking. You're now on the Jack Mytton Way, a new seventy mile route which starts down by the River Severn near Highley and wends across to Llanfair Waterdine. It's intended for horses as well as walkers. Jack Mytton was a hard drinking, hard riding Shropshire squire who

Jack Mytton Way.

Horseshoe sign

famously squandered an inherited fortune at the
beginning of the nineteenth century. So now you
know what you have to do to get your name
commemorated on a walking trail: devote yourself to a life of roistering or robbery.

You won't be able to get up to much mischief   *2km on old rail track.*
along the old railway track, unless you count
going beyond a 'no access' sign as riotous beha-
viour. The Way goes off left here, at the start of a   *Left at sign*
line of poplar trees. Cross a road and zigzag up to
a lane on top of the escarpment. Go immediately   *Right on top of edge*
right through a gap in the hedge. There should be
a Jack Mytton Way sign, but it had disappeared
the last time I did the walk.

The woods cloaking the Edge are below on your
right. Soon you get wide open views to your left
across the inner folds of Wenlock Edge to the Clee
Hills. Out of sight down the slope, Wilderhope
Manor youth hostel is the ideal weekend base for   *1km 750m lane to*
the route.   *lane*

Cross the next lane and go through a gateway
opposite the drive to Wilderhope Manor. Again, I
found the bridleway sign had been broken off.
Now you are walking just inside the woodland,
along a broad track. Just as you're thinking
you've seen enough trees for the day, the woods   *2km in woodland*
open up and you go past a couple of cottages to a
road junction.

Go straight across the junction and through the   *Straight on.*
first gate on the right along an unsurfaced lane,   *Right in 100m.*
past a very des.res. At a gate the bridleway does a   *1km 200m*
dogleg left, but you can cut the corner to a metal
gate and more trees.

Just beyond, the footpath to the south end of the Edge forks left. It's buried in woods for four miles. The Jack Mytton Way dives down the escarpment to Eaton. The creatures which make up the Silurian limestone of Wenlock Edge must have been a glutinous lot. Deep grey mud churned up by horses sucks in your feet to the fetlocks, and sticks on like cement. Come to think of it, I suppose it is the basis for cement.

Geology studies

The lane to Ticklerton will come as a relief after the mud. From here, you can cut a couple of miles off the route by following the Jack Mytton Way to Church Stretton. Turn left then right at successive T-junctions, keep straight on along a path where the lane bends left, then follow J.M. Way signs to the left from Chelmick over Hazler Hill.

1km 750m on lane

Alternative route to Stretton

However, a crossing of Hope Bowdler Hill gives a more interesting finish to the walk, and in any case, people starting at Wenlock need to make the connection to Caradoc.

For the guidebook route, turn right and immediately left in Ticklerton. A footpath goes off to the right three minutes' walk along this road. It mounts pleasantly over pasture, crosses a lane, then forks left down through a belt of trees to Hope Bowdler churchyard. Unfortunately, at the time of writing, summer 1993, there are problems at the village end. The dispute has gone to a public enquiry. So you might prefer to walk along the road for another mile or so. It's quiet and quick.

Right and left in Ticklerton.
Path 250m on right

R.O.W. problems in Hope Bowdler

In Hope Bowdler, turn right along the main road to a wooden gate just beyond a terrace of houses. A wide green trail leads up from here over rolling Hope Bowdler Hill, and descends into the gap

Turn right.
600m on road.
Left at gate

before Caer Caradoc. After a gate, curve left
round the facing hillside to another gate. If you're
at the halfway point, head straight for the outcrop
on Caradoc. If you're going back to Stretton,
swing left again to join the wide track you climbed at the beginning of the walk, and reverse the
first mile and a half of the route.

2km over hill

*Too late for tea? Little
Chef 5km north on
A49*

I have described a clock-wise circuit, but there's a
lot to be said for going the other way round, to
keep the high spots of Caer Caradoc and The
Lawley to the end of the day. This would also
have the advantage of letting you see if the path
problems at Hope Bowdler have been sorted out
before you commit yourself. Try the walk both
ways in different seasons, spring and autumn
perhaps.

MARY WEBB COUNTRY

Long Mynd and the Stiperstones

24mls/38km	8 hrs

Ascent: 3,200ft/975m

The Shropshire hills around Church Stretton were a favourite day destination in my Midland cycling days. It was always a pleasure to top the miniature pass just before the town and see the folds of the Long Mynd in front. I have done very little walking in the area, so I am indebted to a friend from those cycling days for the first part of this route.

OS Landranger Map 137

I am absolving him from responsibility for the second half of the walk as it involves a couple of field sections where the waymarking is almost entirely absent. But don't let that put you off. The route includes both the Long Mynd and the Stiperstones ridge. Even if you are not a Mary Webb enthusiast I think you will still sense the century-blurring atmosphere which influenced her writing, and enjoy the big skies and spacious landscapes.

Yours starting point in All Stretton is so delightful you will be reluctant to stride away. The parking area is at the end of the surfaced section of a tiny road which sneaks up from the village into one of the steep sided hollows that are a feature of the eastern flank of the Long Mynd.

Start at All Stretton GR 455955 Car park Station at Church Stretton

Stroll alongside the steam across two footbridges until you see the jagged tooth of Jonothan's Rock

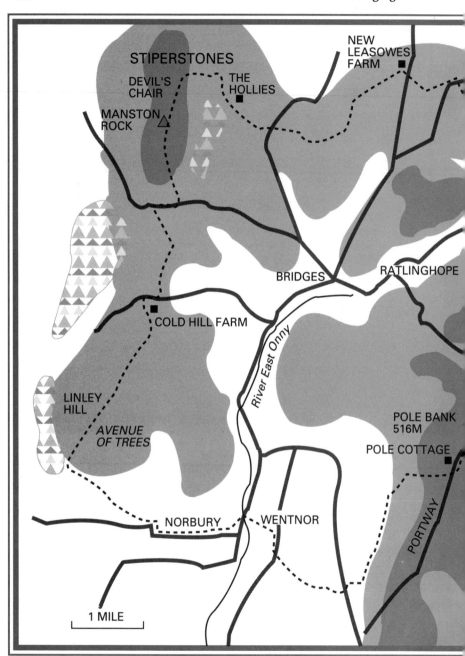

STIPERSTONES

NEW
LEASOWES
FARM

DEVIL'S
CHAIR

THE
HOLLIES

MANSTON
ROCK

BRIDGES

RATLINGHOPE

COLD HILL FARM

River East Onny

LINLEY
HILL

*AVENUE
OF TREES*

POLE BANK
516M

POLE COTTAGE

NORBURY

WENTNOR

PORTWAY

1 MILE

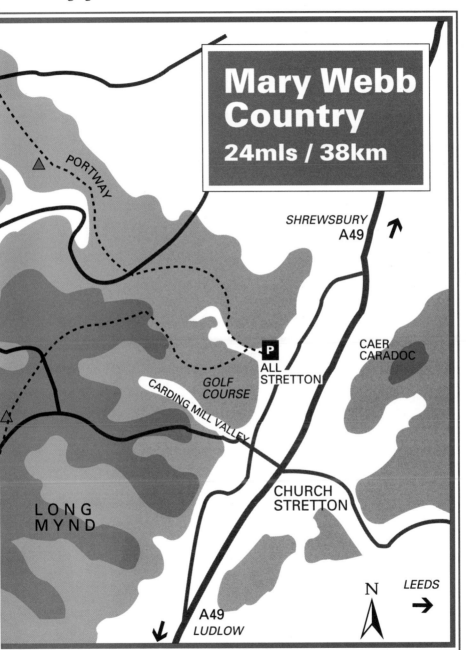

Mary Webb Country
24mls / 38km

PORTWAY

SHREWSBURY
A49

CAER
CARADOC

P
ALL
STRETTON

GOLF
COURSE

CARDING MILL VALLEY

CHURCH
STRETTON

LONG
MYND

A49
LUDLOW

N

LEEDS

topping the hill in front. Near an isolated thorn tree a stony trail hairpins up the hillside. At the top you are on short turf that is marvellously relaxing to walk on. As you head up the hill the views open up around you. To the left, great expanses of heather crown the steep green flanks of the hollows. To the right, the flat farmlands of north Shropshire shimmer into distant Cheshire. There is a feeling of health and vigour which, you will remember from Walk Two, I find lacking in the Western Peak District.

Keep parallel to a fence and you should meet a road opposite a track that drops down a sharp bank then levels out through a gate above a belt of trees. This is part of the Portway, an ancient highway running the length of the Long Mynd.   *GR 434967*

The track stays on top of the grassy ridge, giving you new views south and west, where you will be walking later in the day. Opposite a trig point, go right at a gate and keep on along the fence to a partly surfaced road between hedges. At a T-junction with a lane, turn left, then right at the first stile. Keep going in the same direction across a great prairie of a hillside and as you crest the skyline you will see a stile in a fence. A trail drops down from here through gorse bushes on to a lane at New Leasowes farm.   *5km on Portway*   *300m on lane*

Turn left and immediately right along a lane which soon loses its surface. At a sharp right-hand turn, go straight on through a gate on to a green shelf trail. This curves round the shoulder of the hill and gives you expansive views of your target, the Stiperstones ridge.   *600m*

At a T-junction with a road, turn left and first right up a lane to The Hollies farm. Go through a

gate on to the hillside, then right at a prominent
sign, joining the Shropshire Way up to another
gate. Fork diagonally left up to the top of the
ridge and left again on top.

Buzzard sign

As always on this walk, the views are far-reach-
ing. You should be able to pick out the distinctive
outline of the Arans in the waves of 'blue remembered hills' – to quote another writer – that fade
away into the west.

The outcrops which pierce the ridge are, so the
information boards say, composed of sedimentary
rock 480 million years old. Best known is the
Devil's Chair, said to be occupied when the cloud
is down, as readers of Mary Webb will know.
Next outcrop going south is Manston Rock, with
its unfortunately placed trig point.

Manston Rock 536m

The path along the ridge is a real ankle-wrecker,
but it relents for grassy slopes down to a car park.
Now you know why there were so many people
by the Stiperstones.

On the map, a right of way cuts off through a
ruined gate opposite the car park. It leads you to
a group of ramshackle buildings with no apparent
way through. When I was sorting out the route I
had to return to the road. A sign on the farm gate
issues the invitation to 'Enter at your own risk'.

So I suggest you stay on the lane to a stile. Not
that the line from here is much more clear. Keep a
hedge on your right and head downhill over
another stile and through a buttercup meadow to
a soggy-edged ditch. Find the driest crossing then
aim for a dip in the skyline. On top, hop across
two stiles and veer left along the eastern flank of
the ridge. Keep at the same descending angle on

*Turn right on lane for
500m then left over
stile*

the open hillside and don't be lured by a gate below you bearing a footpath arrow. You will arrive at a stile in a corner where hedges meet. Take the obvious line down through fields to a gate, and via a track to a road.

Turn right to Cold Hill Farm, then left round the back of the house to a stile. Follow the fence on your left to a gap, go left then immediately straight up a steep grassy slope to a stile just below the skyline. Cross the stile and head diagonally left to the brow of the hill, where a clump of trees will come into sight.

Turn right for 200m then left

Beyond the trees, as you gradually descend the broad back of Linley Hill, you are treated to more long-ranging views to the south across the rolling hills of the Marches. Closer to hand, on the right, is the wooded valley of the River West Onny.

Shropshire Way signs

Now you enter an avenue of glorious mature beech trees. According to a local guide book, the avenue was planted by unemployed ex-soldiers after the Napoleonic wars, as a workfare scheme. *Plus ça change* . . . It's good to see that young trees have been planted to fill gaps.

At a gate the beech avenue becomes more densely hemmed in by trees. Turn left over a stile just after the gate to go along the back of a farm, then follow a line of stiles to emerge on to a track which takes you into Norbury.

Turn left at GR 352937 3km from Cold Hill Farm

In the village go left and immediately right round the typical Marches church, with its squat shingled spire. The road bends sharply right at the foot of a slight hill. After the bend take the narrow lane that goes left and follow it to a wider road just short of the hill top village of Wentnor.

Pub in Norbury

1km 500m on lane

Turn left over the bridge then immediately right up a broad trail which climbs to the village.

Turn right in Wentnor, round a couple of bends, and out into fields again. You now have to find the start of a right of way which will take you across a mile or so of fields to the lane which flanks the Long Mynd, whose bulk now fills the horizon. Waymarking is absent but I think the following route doesn't stray too far from the right of way. I have told Shropshire County Council about the problem, so complain to them not me if there are still no signs when you do the walk.

Turn right at T-junction

Go through the second gate on the left after leaving the village. you will see a stile in the fence on the far side of the large sloping field. Cross this and head for a point about two-thirds of the way down the hedge on the left-hand side of the next field. Go over a stile here to an elaborate wooden bridge over a brook. After the bridge, a very indistinct trod goes left and almost immediately right along a hedge. Cross a sort of stile and head diagonally across the next field to white painted iron railings.

Leave lane at GR 385925

These are part of a bridge over another stream. The decking of steel mesh is very rusty and sagged under my modest weight. I advise you to keep your feet on the side girders. Go through a gate diagonally left and cross the next field to a stile in the far right-hand corner, to the lane. I don't enjoy getting snarled up in fields, and a herd of frisky bullocks gave me extra problems when I walked across. But with instructions to follow you should find the route straightforward. It's certainly easy walking from now on.

Dangerous bridge

Turn left on the lane and immediately right up an   *Left and right*
unsurfaced road. At the top you meet the brid-
leway which slips along the foot of the hillside.   *Left on bridleway*
Turn left and follow the way until it becomes a
tarmac lane. At the first gate on the right after this *1km 200m to fork*
point, fork right up onto a wide stony trail which
clambers to the top of the Long Mynd.

You emerge on to the summit road by Pole Cot-   *250m on road*
tage, an unromantic corrugated iron shed. You
don't stay long on the road. A wide trail, signpos-
ted the Jack Mytton Way forks left, and takes you   *Pole Bank 516m*
over Pole Bank, the highest point on the Mynd.

Keep on the trail across a road to a three-way   *2km to junction*
split. If you are early enough, turn sharp right
down into the Carding Mill Valley for tea in   *Fork right at*
Church Stretton. Otherwise, fork right over a   *GR 427958*
slight rise to where a track goes off on the right,
by a small cairn. Follow this path along the hill-   *Turn right in 900m*
side until you see where you can drop steeply
down to a gate on to a golf course.

From the gate the path goes diagonally left. At a   *Left after gate*
post carrying yellow arrows, go left again and   *Left at arrow*
down a steep hillside by a rivulet to a green shelf
trail. This takes you along a side valley on to your
morning route just a few minutes away from your
car.

CLWYD CRESTS

An easy-going ridge trail

30mls/48km   10 hrs
Ascent: 4,560ft/1,390m *or:*

22¹/₂mls /36km   8 hrs
Ascent: 3,675ft/1,120m

The Clwyd ridge presents a striking silhouette that looks far more mountainous than its modest height suggests. A traverse of its fifteen mile length is an obvious target for all hill walkers. It's a switch back belvedere on an easy path which gives constant views extending from the Berwyns to Snowdonia.

The problem is - how do you get back to your starting point without transport? This route solves that problem, taking you along the best part of the ridge and introducing you to some very attractive countryside on the eastern edge of the Alyn valley. There are shorter versions, too, that are walkable in winter daylight.

OS Landranger Map 116

The starting point at Loggerheads Country Park is very easily accessible, now that the Mold by-pass has been built. There's a smart new café and tourist information centre, but I must admit to a nostalgia for the old wooden verandah-style building, put up by the Crosville Motor Company in the thirties and very reminiscent of the days of charabancs and cycling clubs.

Start at Loggerheads GR 198627 Pay car park

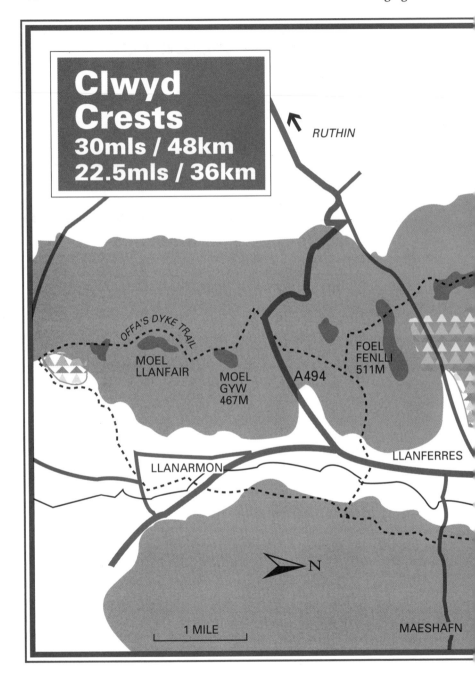

Clwyd Crests
30mls / 48km
22.5mls / 36km

RUTHIN

OFFA'S DYKE TRAIL

MOEL
LLANFAIR

MOEL
GYW
467M

A494

FOEL
FENLLI
511M

LLANFERRES

LLANARMON

N

MAESHAFN

1 MILE

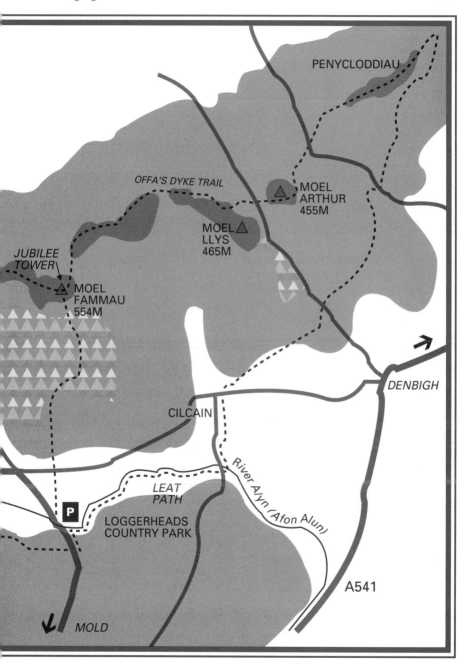

PENYCLODDIAU

OFFA'S DYKE TRAIL

MOEL
ARTHUR
455M

MOEL
LLYS
465M

JUBILEE
TOWER

MOEL
FAMMAU
554M

DENBIGH

CILCAIN

River Alyn (Afon Alun)

LEAT
PATH

P

LOGGERHEADS
COUNTRY PARK

A541

MOLD

The name Loggerheads originates with a boundary dispute between the Lordships of Llanferres and Mold in the eighteenth century. Presumably the lead deposits under the limestone cliffs on the eastern bank of the Alyn river were in contention. A stone memorial on the road side just before you drop down to the country park records the fixing of the boundary at that point in 1763. Don't bother to stop the car because you are going to walk back up the hill to the stone to start the route.

500m from car park

Opposite, a signpost points the way to Maeshafn, whose youth hostel is an ideal weekend base for the walk. The broad path soon takes you on to tarmac. Follow the yellow arrows carefully through Coromandel school, an outdoor centre for the Liverpool education authority. This leads you to a wood of birch and holly trees, and on to a lane below Maeshafn village.

Cross road to path

Keep to official route

Turn left up the hill, then right along a private road through woodland. At a gate on the left, turn on to a ride through beech woods. It's particularly attractive along here in the autumn, when the leaves are turning colour. Keep at the same level until you drop down sharply into a miniature valley.

100m up hill
400m to turn

1km 500m from gate

Short Route

This is the point where you can cut off the southern triangle to reduce the length of the walk by eight miles. Turn right along the valley and cross the infant Alyn by a concrete bridge to the road. Directly in front, a farm road continues up towards the Clwyd ridge. Where the main track dives right through a wall, go straight on, over a

1km to road

1km 300m to fork

gate, to regain the track. Turn left to a wall where you meet the Offa's Dyke Trail at a point where it makes a right-angled turn up the hillside.

300m to Offa's Dyke Trail

Long Route

Instead of turning right down the valley, squiggle your way round to a narrow lane – the snow-drops that once were here have been obliterated under a new house. Don't be tempted by a ladder stile which almost immediately leads off on the left. The path takes you steeply upwards to lime-stone pavements better explored when you have more time.

Go round old cottage

Follow the lane to where it bends sharp right by a bungalow. A path goes straight on along the edge of woodland to a bridleway. Turn left, then right through a gate. A broad green trail contours the hillside to a lane-head. Continue along this lane to a junction at a cottage. A bridleway leads on opposite, gets briefly lost in a field, then is tightly enclosed down to a road. Cross directly over the lane, then a bridge, bear left across a field and you are in Llanarmon.

400m on lane

1km 200m to junction

1km 100m to village

Go into the centre of the village, round the church. Opposite the west gable, a signpost points over a stone stile to Nurse Fawr. The path takes you across fields to a lane-head. Keep walking in the same direction along a track past a farm. You go through a wood and join the Offa's Dyke Trail at an open common. You must turn very sharply back right here, along the other side of the wood, otherwise you will be on your way to Chepstow.

Join Offa's Dyke Trail at GR 171543

There's not much I need to tell you about the route along the ridge. Offa's Dyke Trail signs provide continuous waymarking. At Clwyd Gate, where the Trail crosses the main Rhuthun road, you have to do a short sidestep to the right. Immediately after turning off the road again, a dotted line on your map leads directly up to the hill-crest. Access to it is firmly barricaded, and Clwyd County Council tell me the right of way was extinguished several years ago. It emphasises how constantly alert we have to be.

250m on road

The official Trail stays at the lower level. Look out for the left-hand fork off the farm road, through a belt of trees. Just beyond, you are at the right-angle turn where the two routes join.

*Routes meet at
GR 173596*

Joint Route

Walk up to the ridge over grass. As this is the Clwyd Crests walk, leave the signed trail temporarily to top out on Foel Fenlli, the first of the three Iron Age hill forts on the ridge. Drop down to the car park at Bwlch Penbarra, then take the upper of two paths, which climbs steadily up to Moel Fammau, highest point on the ridge.

Foel Fenlli 511m

Moel Fammau 534m

This section of the ridge is popular with strollers and with fell runners, as the gradients are just steep enough to test both. The Jubilee Tower on the summit of Moel Fammau is the target of most of the casual walkers. It was built to commemorate the jubilee of George III, and was originally 115 feet high, but it collapsed fifty years later, in 1862.

Have fun picking out the Snowdonia summits from the skyline map engraved on a plate on top of the tower. In the winter they are covered in snow surprisingly often.

Jubilee Tower

The next dip in the ridge is crossed by a slender   *Moel Arthur 455m*
lane that clambers up just before Moel Arthur, the
second hill fort. The Trail circles round to the
right, but your route cuts across to the top. The
grassy banks of the old fort make handy back
rests for lunch, if you are walking the shorter
route. After another lane crossing, you finish off
the ridge section with the short turf of Penycloddiau hill fort.

Now you're turning for home, don't expect a   *Turn back at*
stroll along easy paths, at least not until Cilcain.   *GR 121689*
There are some tiring little ups and downs hidden
on this eastern flank of the Clwyds. The County
Council has recently improved the waymarking
on this sequence of paths.

At the turning point, go back sharply along a   *Turn right and right*
farm track but at the first gate bear right through
another gate on to grassland, on the upper side of   *Right in 350m*
a fence. Descend slightly into a miniature cwm.
After a gate the track circles round to the right
but you can cut straight across, along the line of
an old dyke. Go left through a gate then immediately right, keeping between a fence and a
wall. A new stile and tiny bridge take you over to
fields and a farm.

Keep going in the same direction. You drop into   *Straight on*
another side valley through a sequence of stiles.
Cross a stream by a substantial wooden bridge
and climb a steep slope to Pen-y-Bryn farm. More
stiles shunt you to the right, and down into yet
another valley. Leave the field through a gate and
go up the lane immediately opposite to Bryn-
ffynon farm.

A diverted right of way takes you to the left of   *Up hillside*
the buildings. The hillside behind the farm used
to be delightful – mature pasture dotted with
gorse. When I was there last, in May 1993, the
whole slope was being ploughed up. Later the
same day, I saw another hillside suffering the
same fate. When farmers are being paid to take
land out of cultivation, and when they are com-
plaining that low meat prices make the rearing of
lambs uneconomic, I can't understand why hill
land is still vanishing under the plough.

At the top of the slope, pass through a small iron
gate into a vast field. Head diagonally upwards,
to the right of a circular plantation of pines. You
emerge on to a bridleway opposite a gate tempt-
ing you to carry straight on through woodland. In   *Left for 500m then*
fact, the right of way goes left along an avenue of *right*
magnificent trees, mostly beeches, and then turns

back sharp right on itself, past a cottage, to join the path through the wood.

When you leave the south side of the wood, head straight down the hillside between the fence and a superb sycamore. Climb again to cross a lane at stiles, then descend yet again, diagonally left, to a stile in the hedge halfway down the field. Keep on this diagonal line to a stream, which can be crossed easily on a line of stones if you are going the right way. Ignore a sort of stile in front of you – it falls over when you stand on it. Go up the field to the border of woodland, and bear left to a bridleway which runs between high hedges.

Cross lane

GR 168667

The continuation path starts a little to the right, on the near side of a rusting steel skeleton of a barn. Go over stiles to the edge of Gors Farm. The right of way keeps left along a vegetation-choked hollow. You emerge on lanes at a T-junction. Carry on along the lane opposite and straight on again on a path where the lane bends left. This footpath takes you into Cilcain via the sports field.

Right and left

300m on lane

Pub in Cilcain

Turn left in the village, over the crossroads, round bends, down a steep hill, over a narrow bridge, and up the other slope. At the top, a footpath goes back acutely right. This leads you on to an abandoned leat – a narrow canal constructed to deliver continuous supplies of water to the mills involved with the lead mining operations along the Alyn Valley. Dry now, it offers you an enjoy-able balcony walk above the river straight back to Loggerheads Country Park. But don't linger. The café closes soon after five o'clock, and at four in the winter.

1km 500m on road

Leat path 3km long
Strange spelling on
signs!

Two Day Version

An interesting path leads directly from the Country Park to Moel Fammau, enabling you to split the walk into two almost equal lengths. This link is about three miles long.

Turn right immediately outside the car park entrance, along a narrow lane, to a T-junction. A few paces to the right, a footpath signed to Moel Fammau leads off alongside a stream, over fields to the fringe of the forests which cloak the eastern side of the hill here. Turn right, go diagonally across a field to a farm track, turn right again to a stile at the foot of a very steep path. This takes you breathlessly upwards, directly to the Jubilee Tower. You would use this connecting link at the end of the south section and the beginning of the north section.

Challenge Walk

A supported walk following an almost identical route is usually organised in September by the Merseyside group of the LDWA.

BERWYN CHALLENGE

Two sides of the Dee

30mls/48km   10 hrs

Ascent: 3,900ft/1,190m

Many Midlanders get their first taste of hill walking on the Berwyns. I have a photograph of myself at the age of eighteen struggling up the last few feet of Moel Sych, from Llyn Llyncaws – carrying a bicycle. I did realise eventually that it might be easier to leave the bike behind. But on foot I never got beyond a top-and-back short day from any starting point.

OS Landranger Map 125

Writing this guide gave me the incentive to try a route I had long considered – pushing on from Moel Sych across the Milltir Cerig road and circling back along the low hills on the west side of the Dee. There are only two suitable bridges, so Cynwyd had to be the starting point and Llandderfel the southern river crossing point.

Start at Cynwyd GR 056411 Limited parking by post office. Youth hostel

Start up the lane that heads up hill towards the ridge. You have a choice almost immediately. You can keep on the lane and its continuation as a forest track and try to find the Fford Saeson, an ancient hill crossing. But last time I tried this I ended up wading through deep heather.

The easier and pleasanter alternative is to fork right at a gate, past a tiny reservoir and along the floor of the valley. Where the track does a U-turn at the far edge of the forest, bear right, then go left at a gate on to a less worn trail which fades

Turn right in 1km 200m

Track starts at GR 092389

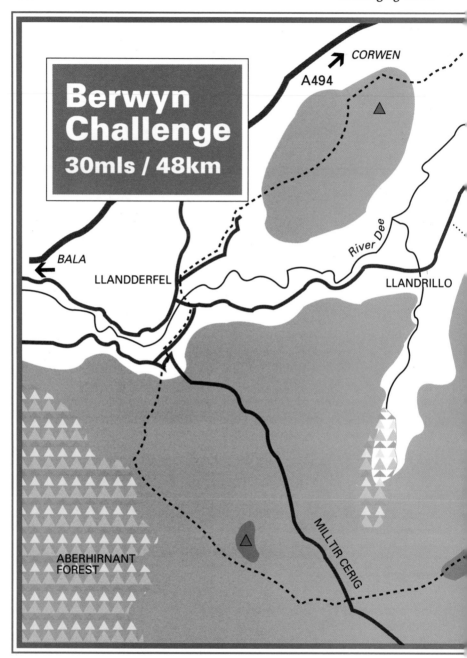

CORWEN

A494

BALA

LLANDDERFEL

River Dee

LLANDRILLO

ABERHIRNANT
FOREST

MILLTIR CERIG

**Berwyn
Challenge**
30mls / 48km

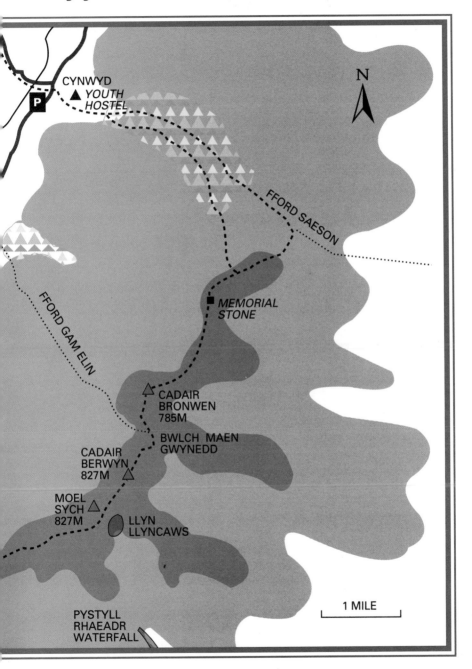

CYNWYD
▲ YOUTH
  HOSTEL

P

N

FFORD SAESON

FFORD GAM ELIN

■ MEMORIAL
  STONE

△ CADAIR
  BRONWEN
  785M

BWLCH MAEN
GWYNEDD

CADAIR
BERWYN
827M △

MOEL
SYCH △
827M

LLYN
LLYNCAWS

1 MILE

PYSTYLL
RHAEADR
WATERFALL

out just short of the ridge. Judging by the boot prints, this seems to be a well-used approach although it is not shown as a right of way on the map.

GR 092389

On top, you need to turn positively right. A thin squelchy trod follows the line of a fence and takes you on to a low rise. Go left here and descend to the trail that crosses the Berwyns from Llanarmon. A plaque set into a rock commemorates Wayfarer, a writer whose accounts of exploring the Welsh hills on a bicycle were very popular in the thirties.

GR 091366

You can be sure of legal access from now on. A sign records that a permissive path exists all along the ridge. It's decorated with occasional ladder stiles that keep you on the straight and narrow.

Cader Bronwen is your first top, before you drop to where another ancient hill track, the Fford Gam Elin, crosses the ridge at the Bwlch Maen Gwynedd. After the stile at the Bwlch, cross over to the eastern rim. The path is drier underfoot, and you get the benefit of dramatic views into the cliff-edged cwm as you climb towards Cader Berwyn.

Cader Bronwen 785m/2572ft

Cader Berwyn 827m/2712ft

On my old one-inch map, Moel Sych is just one foot higher than Cader Berwyn. It's usually been the point where I get out my sandwiches and while away an hour before I turn back down to the valley. For the guidebook route I pressed on into unknown territory.

Moel Sych 827m/2713ft

A sign at a ladder stile points the way to the Milltir Cerig, the most direct road pass between Shrewsbury and Bala. In my cycle racing days, my club used to have an annual early season training ride from Birmingham to Beddgelert, for the weekend. The long ascent of the Milltir Cerig was an opportunity to test hill climbing fitness.

The Berwyns

The walk from Moel Sych turns out to be a bit of a test too. It seems much longer than measurement on a map suggests. A series of low crests keep on deceiving you into thinking the road crossing is just in front. If you managed to keep your feet dry up to Moel Sych, you certainly won't now.

5km 500m squelch

But all good things come to an end, and eventually you walk on to tarmac. The way ahead doesn't look any more promising, with no path apparent across a marsh. Be brave. Go straight on

to the corner of a fence and follow it to cross
another fence at a sort of stile.   *250m*

A few paces on the other side of the fence will
take you to a trace of a green trail going right.
Follow this up the hillside and round to the left,
where it drops you into the hollow of a much
more defined path. Turn right again, cross a rickety stile and wade through a very wet bog.

You're on open hillside now, aiming to cross the   *Cross ridge at*
ridge just to the left of the highest point. Unfor- *GR 997308*
tunately the path gets itself lost in the heather.
When you start to descend the western side, you
need to head for the highest corner of Aberhirnant Forest, diagonally right. A heather-covered
shelf makes a bee line towards this point. An
alternative is to abandon attempts to stay on the
right of way and to cross the ridge at the highest
point, from which a sort of path descends.

Once you get near the top corner of the forest, the
path becomes much more obvious. There are even
signs. Soon you are contouring along a sunken
green trail above the attractive Hirnant valley.   *Bwlch-y-Fenni*
When you go through a gate on to a farm road   *GR 972333*
the worst terrain is all behind you. I hope you
will allow me a slightly sadistic smile at the
thought of you following in my wet footsteps
from Moel Sych. These are supposed to be challenging walks you know!

Enjoy almost two miles downhill on a firm sur-   *Right for 200m*
face. At the road turn right round the hairpin   *footpath sign*
bend, then left down by a bungalow on to a field
path that takes you on to the main valley road.
After the Berwyns, you won't mind a short stretch
of tarmac and anyway there are some fine mature   *1km 200m on road*
trees to admire on your right.

Facing the left turn over the river bridge to Llandderfel there is an attractive looking inn. I thought
I had arranged my timing to perfection by arriv-
ing there just after six o'clock – one of the few
advantages of starting at half past eleven. But a
sign on the door gave the opening time as 7.00pm
on Fridays. It was the last Friday in April. So I sat
on the bridge over the Dee, scoffed a Mars Bar,
swigged the last of my carbohydrate drink, and
trotted off along the lane to Llandderfel village.

*Turn left at
GR 984365 over
bridge*

*Turn right at first road
after bridge*

This side of the Dee is a soft contrast to the
bareness of the Berwyn ridge. It's a good example
of the point I made in the introduction to the
guide, that the need to make up a complete circuit
can take you through some delightful countryside
you might otherwise not visit.

Turn right in Llandderfel village, then fork left at
the top of a rise. I could sing the next instructions
– if I could sing. Keep right on to the end of the
road, following it up round several bends through
a pastoral landscape, ablaze with gorse bloom
when I was there. On that April evening, many
sheep with their little lambs passed me by on the
road. I'm sure I heard a choir.

*Turn right in 500m,
left in 200m*

*2km 500m on lane to
GR 998387*

After the gate at the end of the road, the surface
changes to a rough track between high banks.
Fork right opposite an isolated cottage up a rise to
a gate. Go through the gate and turn sharp left
along the fence. This will take you to a trail which
continues to the right up a shallow valley.

Turn right in 200m

300m to gate
Left for 100m

You emerge on to wide open grassland and pass
through another gate. Keep straight on along the
flat top of the hill until the trail descends gently to
a stream. From here there is an obvious track
between a stone wall and a plantation. At the end

1km 500m along top

600m by wood

of the wood turn sharp right following a brid-
leway sign which points you across fields to a   *Lanehead*
lane-head. It's just a matter now of walking down   *GR 026414*
the lanes to Cynwyd, turning right at the T-
junction, right again and immediately left.   *4km to finish*

My pint of cool cider at the village pub tasted all
the better for the two hour wait.

BETWS LAKES AND FORESTS

The softer side of Snowdonia

20mls/32km   8 hrs
Ascent: 3,280ft/1,000m *or:*

17mls/27km   7 hrs
Ascent: 2,130ft/650m

I'm very fortunate in being able to get to the heart of Snowdonia in an hour and a half, courtesy of the new expressway along the North Wales coast. I often end my day on the Welsh hills with a pot of tea in Betws-y-coed, sitting in the sun near the railway station looking out across the little town's attractive green heart at the wooded crags. At the risk of upsetting Welsh patriots, I will suggest that the atmosphere is almost alpine.

OS Landranger Map 115

But as well as being a very pleasant place to round off the day, Betws can also be the start of walks that offer a contrast to hill-top expeditions. The maze of woods and lakes to the northwest of Betws is particularly attractive. There are many alternative ways to explore, but my suggested route give you an introduction to the area and the option of including the traverse of a rocky ridge. The walk is especially appealing in spring and autumn.

Start at Betws-y-Coed GR 795566 Parking by railway station

From the station, walk up the main street and turn right across the bridge opposite Climber &

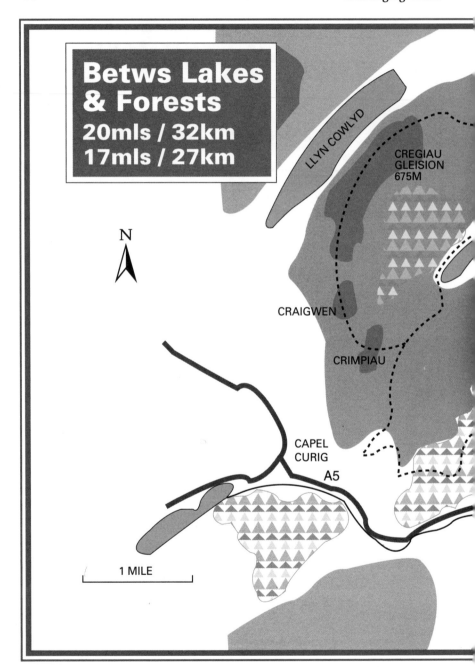

Betws Lakes & Forests
20mls / 32km
17mls / 27km

LLYN COWLYD

CREGIAU GLEISION 675M

N

CRAIGWEN

CRIMPIAU

CAPEL CURIG

A5

1 MILE

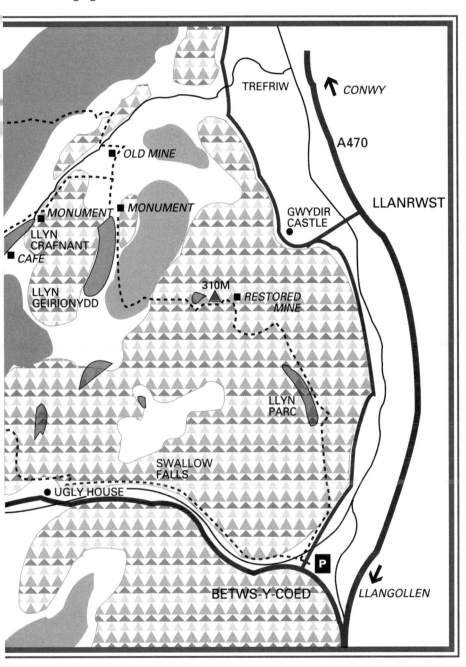

Rambler. Don't get lured inside – you can look at
the latest gear on the way back. Over the bridge,
go immediately left and walk up a slight rise to
where a road goes off right by a guest house. This   *200m from bridge*
takes you straight on to a forest track which
climbs gradually. On top of the hill a narrow path   *600m*
signed for Walks 7 and 8 leads off on the left
through trees above a stream.

You emerge by an open meadow with a cottage   *1km 200m*
on the far side, then meet a major forest track.
Turn right to where you have a choice of three
ways. The right-hand and centre trails take you
down to Gwydyr Uchaf chapel and a tiny gated
lane round to Llyn Geirionydd.

Llyn Geirionydd

You are keeping to the heart of the forest, going left above Llyn Parc to a dip between two wooded slopes where you again have a choice of trails. Fork left, signed Walk 8, and descend steeply to where the track gains a hard surface. Take the second forest road on the left, which curves round to meet another narrow lane almost opposite old mine buildings, recently tidied up.

Fork left

Fork left in 1km

Left in 600m

Left on lane

Turn left on the lane and you will see a fenced-in path, probably with a 'no mountain bikes' sign, going up by the side of the old walls. The sign is superfluous, as there are umpteen steps to clamber up before the path exits on to a forest track above the old mine buildings.

You will see another stile in front of you, where the forest track swings left. It takes you on to a wide green trail heading straight up the hill. Ignore the stiles on the right, cross a rickety stile on the path itself, and another stile to a lane opposite a cottage. If you are keen on collecting tops, there's a trig point on your right.

Go down the path on the left-hand side of the cottage and along a forest trail to the side of a small lake. From the further end of its embankment bear left, cross two stiles and swing right behind the remains of one more mine. A stile takes you on to open hillside and your first view of Llyn Geirionydd.

It might not be as large as Windermere or Coniston – and is certainly harder to pronounce! – but its setting between wooded hills rivals any Cumbrian lake. The path heads diagonally down to the waterside. Stroll along the lane to the northern end of the lane and turn left through an iron gate. The shore line boulders offer a seat with a view for your morning stop.

3km from first mine

Beyond the end of the lake on a low rise a
crumbling monument pillar acts as a cairn for the
route. Follow a wide green trail to a wall. On the
other side the path divides and you have to make
your choice between circling above Llyn Crafnant
on the hill tops, or keeping down by the lakeside.
Each route offers its own pleasures, and the two
join again at the southern end of the lake.

*Time to make your
choice*

Longer Route

Bear right down the hillside through open woodland. There's supposed to be a path going off left,
but you will almost certainly find yourself down
by yet more ruined mine buildings above a
stream. Turn left on the lower side of the buildings across the remains of spoil heaps, heading for
an area obviously used for training horses. Walk
along the top of a bank to a bridge over the Afon
Crafnant and gain the road.

1km from monument

Just to the right a hard surfaced track slants up
the facing hillside, then hairpins back towards
Lledwigan farm. Signs direct you round the farm
on to open hillside. The path is going to Llyn
Cowlyd, but you must turn left where it crosses
the ridge at a fence. Follow the fence along a
boggy flat section to the rocks of Creigiau Gleision.

2km to top

This is the start of three delectable miles over
miniature mountains, with views of the major
Snowdonia peaks as a bonus. On the right, sheer
cliffs plunge down to Llyn Cowlyd. Then you
swing south on to more grassy hill slopes.

*Creigiau Gleision
675m*

The flat bwlch before you climb up to Craig-wen
is always very wet. A rocky spur on the left

Craig-wen 539m

tempts you up to do some bouldering then you drop down again before the last steep little ascent to Crimpiau, a sort of full stop at the end of this hill crest excursion. Descend to the wide trail immediately below.

Crimpiau 539m

Short Route

From the dividing point of the routes contour round the shoulder of the hill and join a forestry road, which brings you on to a lane near a car park. On a short winter day, you could do the circuit of the Crafnant tops from here. Walk up the lane to the lake and fork right by the monument which commemorates the gift of the lake to the people of Llanrwst.

You are on a forest trail along the northern side of the lake. The lane continues on the southern side. Halfway down the lake you will see a cottage on the opposite side with parked cars and boats nearby. It's an anglers' café but I know you wouldn't want to suffer road walking just to get a pot of tea. Or would you?

At the end of the lake the forest track starts to rise, and the surface becomes more stony. A path leads off to the left around a cottage and on to a wider trail which climbs up to the bwlch below Crimpiau. If you succumbed to the temptations of the café, a trail leads up from the road head.

3km from monument

Joint Route

The trail is the main walkers' pass between the Conway Valley and Capel Curig. Just above Capel it converges with another track which cuts back

GR 733582

sharply to an isolated farm. I avoid the doubling
back by cutting straight across the ridge when the   *Cut-across at*
trail swings right.   *GR 736586*

Follow the boggy track from the farm down
towards Pont Cyfyng, but just after the first gate   *500m*
turn left by a pile of stones. You will crest a low
rise and find yourself near a ladder stile over a
wall.

Slither down through a birch wood to a tiny
stream, climb the facing slope on a more defined
path between a fence and a wall, and you will be
back at the edge of the main forest. Don't continue between the fence and the wall. Clamber
over a gate on to a wide forest track and follow
this round a big horseshoe bend until you are   *2km 500m in forest*
behind a farm above the Capel-Betws road.

A gate opens to a farm road. Where it turns right,
almost immediately, turn left past a bungalow,
across a stream to a narrow path which takes you
to the lane from the Ugly House. Turn right down   *Right down lane*
the hill and left along another forest trail.   *Turn left in 200m*

Take the first right fork and you will have the   *Fork right in 200m*
pleasant surprise of discovering you are poised
above the Afon Llugwy where it thunders over
the Swallow Falls. You're getting a fine view of
the Falls without paying. That's almost enough in
itself to make the walk worth doing.

If you want to get back to Betws quickly, walk up
on to the road. But it's pleasanter to meander
along the riverside path, which delivers you   *3km from Swallow*
directly to the bridge.   *Falls*

THE CARNEDD COLLECTION

High days in Snowdonia

30mls/48km $10^1/_2$ hrs
Ascent: 6,000ft/1,830m *or:*

22 mls/35km   8 hrs
Ascent: 4,500ft/1,370m

The Carnedds offer the longest high level walk in Snowdonia. But, as with the Clwyd and Berwyn ridges, it is difficult to get back to your starting point after an end-to-end traverse without retracing your footsteps. I'm going to suggest a solution. Two in fact. The longer route enables you to collect all the Carnedd tops in one day, with only a short return excursion. The less-long route omits the Dafydd spur but still offers a satisfying high circuit.

OS Landranger Map 115

The two common factors for both routes are a start at the far north of the range, and a ten-minute bus ride to close the circuit, on one of these handy Sherpa minibuses. You start at the village of Roewen, just south of Conway. The only parking space is at the lower end of the village near a small housing estate. A large group of people would be well advised to leave as many cars as possible in an official car park in Conway.

Start at Roewen GR 761719 Limited parking Youth Hostel

Walk up through the village to a right turn signposted to the youth hostel. The gradient is very steep, so don't be tempted to drive up here unless you are staying at the hostel. Beyond the hostel you're on a pleasant green trail until you con-

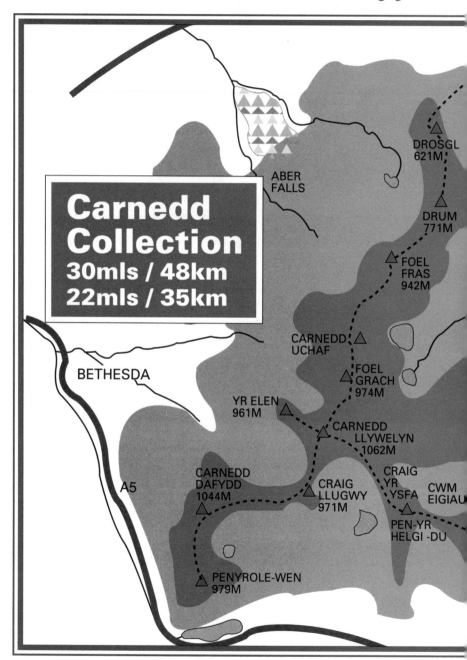

Carnedd Collection
30mls / 48km
22mls / 35km

ABER FALLS

DROSGL 621M

DRUM 771M

FOEL FRAS 942M

CARNEDD UCHAF

FOEL GRACH 974M

BETHESDA

YR ELEN 961M

CARNEDD LLYWELYN 1062M

CRAIG YR YSFA

CWM EIGIAU

A5

CARNEDD DAFYDD 1044M

CRAIG LLUGWY 971M

PEN-YR HELGI -DU

PENYROLE-WEN 979M

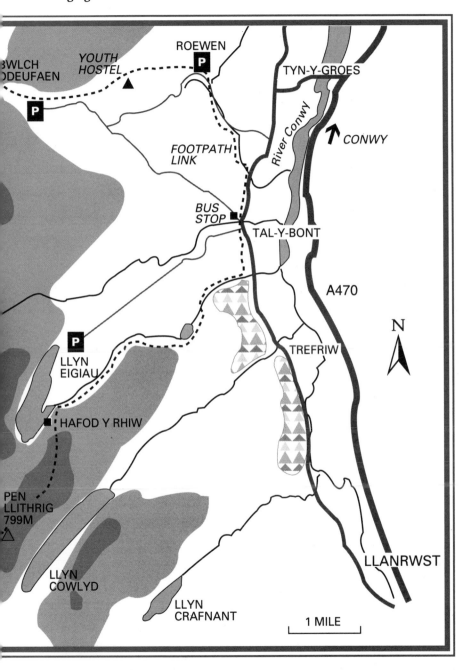

verge with a lane again for a mile to a road-head *6km from start*
car park. If you could manage to find all-day *Bwlch-y-Ddeufaen*
parking at the finishing village, Tal-y-Bont, you
could shorten the walk by organising a shuttle of
cars.

Go through the gate at Bwlch-y-Ddeufaen and
turn left alongside the stone wall. You start to
climb immediately to your first top of the day. *Drosgl 621m*
Below you on your right a wide track scars up to
join you for the final slopes of the next top, Drum, *Drum 771m*
with its sheltering round of stones.

Ahead is Foel Fras, the first three thousander on *Foel Fras 942m*
the ridge, to use traditional measurement. It's a
steady slog up to its flat stony top. But if you're
doing the longer route you will stay around the *Carnedd Uchaf*
same height for the next eight miles. Not surprisingly, it's a favourite haunt for fell runners.

There's very little more height to gain for the next *Foel Grach 974m*
tops, and even the last bouldery slopes of Car- *Carnedd Llywelyn*
nedd Llywelyn should not delay you long. This is *1062m*
the highest point of the route, and the moment at
which the decision has to be made on the distance.

If you want to collect all the Carnedd tops you *Yr Elen 961m*
have to nip out to Yr Elen, then contour back *Carnedd Dafydd*
under Carnedd Llywelyn along the spur to Car- *1044m*
nedd Dafydd and Penyrole-wen, picking up Craig *Penyrole-wen 979m*
Llugwy on the way. If you choose the shorter *Craig Llugwy 971m*
route you will still have a magnificent mountain
day, and perhaps a little more time and energy to
enjoy it.

Whether you have been along the spur or not, the
next section of the route takes you down the bare
east flank of Llywelyn to the rock ridge of Craig-

yr-ysfa. Keep close to the edge and you will probably see climbers on the sheer walls of an amphitheatre.

It's an entertaining scramble down to Bwlch Eryl Farchog, a sharp little col, if I am allowed to mix languages. I will never forget the first time I was here. In fact, it was my first time on the Carnedds and my first long Welsh route on a snow-and-ice plastered Great Gully, in the centre of Craig-yr-ysfa.

For reasons too complicated to go into here, I had reversed the lower half of the climb in the dark. I thrashed up from Cwm Eigiau through deep soft snow, and stepped out of shadow into brilliance on top of the col. Ogwen, Tryfan and the Glyders were spread out in front of me, smothered in snow and bathed in moonlight. It is a scene that is fixed in my memory like a photographic image.

I'm sure the sun will be shining for your day on the Carnedds. The nose of Penyrhelgi-du in front is not a serious obstacle. Keep to the right at first, then move back to the top of the rocks. The summit is flat so your attention can stray to the last top of the day, Pen Lithrig. You have to drop down to Bwlch Tremarchog and clamber most of the way back up again. It's a teasing little ascent too, with several false tops.

Penyrhelgi-du 833m

Pen Lithrig 799m

From the summit, turn ninety degrees left and descend to a boggy moor. Keep to the right-hand edge, looking over Llyn Cowlyd to the cliffs of Creigiau Gleision you walked along on the Betws Lakes route. You'll find a tenuous trod which avoids the worst of the wet. When you come up against a low crag at the north end turn left along a new fence, and eventually you will find yourself on a cross trail that will take you past Hafod-y-Rhiw cottage.

When the trail divides, just past the cottage, take the right-hand branch. The other goes to road-head parking used by people walking the short Cwm Eigiau horseshoe. You have an old road underfoot now, at first almost flat, then gently descending into open woodland and past a small reservoir to join a roughly surfaced road.

4km from Hafod-y-Rhiw

Turn left, under a pipeline, and across a bridge. As the lane starts to rise, you will see a ladder stile on the right. This takes you on to a direct path to Tal-y-bont, through bluebell woods and past waterfalls. It's a delightful end to the day.

Yellow arrows
Left on lane to village

You make the final link back to Roewen by Sherpa bus. There's one conveniently timed for ten to six, and a last chance bus at ten to eight. The bus stop is by the pub. If you insist on completing the circuit on foot, walk along the main road to a bridge, turn left at footpath sign by the Afon Roe, then join a lane to Roewen. It's about three miles.

Get timetable at tourist offices in Betws or Conway

WELSH 3000ft PEAKS PLUS!

The most challenging walk in Wales

30mls/48km   15 hrs

Ascent: 12,500ft/3,800m

I hadn't fully appreciated the current level of interest in this famous traverse of all the three-thousand-feet peaks in Wales until a couple of summers ago. I started at dawn from Pen y Pass in the company of several dozen others and met at least the same number of people on their way down over Crib Goch. At five o'clock in the morning, the ridge was crowded with two queues of scramblers trying to go in opposite directions. I don't think anyone got shouldered off.

On that occasion, I was fortunate to be with the LDWA Staffordshire Group. Their support party provided a cooked breakfast at Nant Peris, and a lunch of salad sandwiches and tinned peaches at Ogwen. Such high living is not conducive to fast times, but it doesn't half ease the pain. I shall always remember drifting along the Carnedd ridge at the end of the day, looking out across a sea turned to liquid gold by the setting sun.

But let's go back to the beginning of the story. There used to be fourteen 3,000 feet peaks, but a fifteenth has mysteriously appeared on the Car-neddau. Their traverse in one day was probably pioneered by the Rucksack Club in the early twenties, and was popularised in the thirties by Thomas Firbank in his book '*I Bought a Mountain*', the story of his life on a farm near Capel Curig.

OS Landranger Map 115

The list:
Snowdon 3561ft
Garnedd Ugain
(Crib-y-ddysgyl)
2493ft
Crib Goch 3022ft
Elidir Fawr 3033ft
Y Garn 3104ft
Glyder Fawr 3279ft

He and his friends recorded 8 hours 25 minutes, and his wife Esme was only just over an hour slower. Fell runners have since reduced the fastest time to well under five hours. These times were for a first-top-to-last-top distance of about twenty four miles.

Traditionally, the route is tackled from south to north. So you have to start by climbing Snowdon. If you want to get away early, this gives you two practical alternatives, illustrated by that morning meeting on Crib Goch.

First, you can go up the previous evening and bivvy on the summit. Personally, I think that even if you walked up rather than used the mountain railway, you can't claim to have climbed all the three thousand feet peaks in one continuous effort. And anyway, a few hours of uncomfortable dozing is not the best preparation for a long hard day.

The descent is logical, though, over Crib-y-ddys-gyl to Crib Goch and then down its north ridge to Nant Peris. Do check out the drop into the Pass in advance, so you know where to swing left into Cwmglas, to avoid walking off the cliffs of Dinas Mot.

Second, you can start from Pen y Pass and tick off Crib Goch and Crib-y-ddysgyl on the way up Snowdon. But this gives you the problem of finding a way down that doesn't involve retracing your steps. The only realistic answer is to trudge down the railway line to Clogwyn station and slither down precipitous slopes to Nant Peris.

The routes coincide from here. You are faced by a 2,500 feet climb up Elidir Fawr, and rewarded by

Glyder Fach 3262ft
Tryfan 3010ft
Penyrole-wen 3211ft
Carnedd Dafydd 3423ft
Yr Elen 3154ft
Carnedd Llywelyn 3485ft
Foel Grach 3196ft
Carnedd Uchaf (the new top) 3038ft
Foel Fras 3091ft

a delightful traverse of the Glyders to Tryfan. The descent can be made down the west face to a parking bay halfway along Llyn Ogwen, or by a return to Bwlch Tryfan. You now have to gain that lost height all over again, up the notoriously heartbreaking climb of Penyrole-wen. I recommend that you go up the east ridge, rather than the steep nose overlooking Idwal Cottage. So turn right on the road, then left at the east end of the lake.

The crux of the walk!

Once you are on top of the Carneddau, the hard work is over, although you still have to persuade your feet to take you out to Yr Elen before you top out on Carnedd Llywelyn. The final descent is usually made from the saddle between Foel Fras and Drum, to a rough reservoir track and the roadhead above Aber.

That's the way that most people walk the Welsh 3,000s. But I'm going to suggest that you tackle the route in the opposite direction, going from north to south. It's not just because I'm naturally perverse, or even because facing the sun all day gives you a better tan. There are very practical reasons. The two main advantages are that you go down the mountainsides which, in the traditional direction, present the two hardest climbs. And that you don't have to rely on other people to shuttle you back to base, because reliable public transport is available.

The alternative approach

The key is this latter benefit is to approach the Carneddau from the east, rather than from Aber. Roewen Youth hostel makes the ideal night base. From here, walk or drive up to Bwlch y Ddeufaen. This, you will probably recall, is the first part of the Carnedd Collection route. You follow this all the way to Penyrole-wen. There's no need

Start at Bwlch y Ddeufaen GR 716717 Parking Follow main Carneddau ridge

to climb Llywelyn twice, by the way, as you can contour round on the way back from the diversion to Yr Elen.

I advised you to climb Penyrole-wen by the east ridge, but in descent, the south ridge is faster. As you walk along the road from Idwal Cottage, the direct ascent route up Tryfan shows up as a broad scar. Access to the path is at a walled parking bay. If you want to make the day more interesting, you can of course scramble up the north ridge of Tryfan and follow on up Bristly Ridge.

Left on road for 1km

Tryfan path starts from parking area

Descend to Bwlch Tryfan and scrabble up the scree slope to gain the Glyders. The bouldery ridge will slow you a little but when you get beyond Y Garn the ground is easier underfoot. The descent from Elidir Fawr is on grass and then along a broad track.

One of the finest ridge walks in Wales

From Nant Peris, walk up the Llanberis Pass road until you have the climbers' cliff of Carreg Wasted on your left – I've certainly wasted too many hours perched on wrinkles up there – and the amphitheatre of Cwmglas on your right. Cross the bridge over the stream near Blaen y Nant and make your way into the cwm.

3km on road

Right over bridge at GR 623570

It's difficult to give you precise instruction on the safest way up to Crib Goch, which is why I suggested a reconnaissance trip for the descent route if you don't know this mountainside. But you have to get well up the cwm, beyond the cliffs of Dinas Mot, before you swing left to gain the north ridge at a sort of nose. If you have any doubts, carry on up the road to the top of the pass, and climb Crib Goch by the normal path. It won't take you all that much longer. Presumably you are well acquainted with the rest of the route to the summit of Snowdon.

Veer left above Dinas Mot cliffs to Crib Goch north ridge

Usual Horseshoe route to top

Tryfan from Penyrole-wen (photo: Graham Beech)

Let's look forward to that moment when you accomplish the traverse of the Welsh 3,000s, finishing in the most stylish way on the highest summit. You can rest on your laurels and walk back down the tourist path to Pen y Pass. But if you still have some energy left why not outwalk most other three-thousander challengers by continuing round the rest of the Snowdon Horseshoe? Or are your thighs already wincing at the thought of adding that extra climb up Lliwedd?

The 'plus' of the ultimate finish

Whichever way you descend from Snowdon, you will end up at Pen y Pass. I promised that you could get back to base from here by public transport. The last bus of the day on the Llanberis-Llandudno route crosses the top at seven o'clock, and will drop you off at Roewen an hour later. If you are doubtful about finishing the walk by this time, book in at Pen y Pass hostel and bus back to Roewen the next day.

Sherpa bus back to Roewen - but do check current timetable

THE CNICHT CONNECTION

Short but very sweet

20mls/32km   8 hrs
Ascent: 3,450ft/1,050m

It has been said many times that the best views of mountains are obtained from a point mid way in height. If that's true, this route will give you a whole day of perfect vistas. Snowdon and the Glyders will be constantly in your gaze across a foreground of tiny lakes and crags. It is one of the only three linear walks in the guide, but it links up with the Sherpa minibus service.

OS Landranger Map 115

Cnicht is the final target, but Moel Siabod is the first and major summit. The most direct route goes up the ridge from Pont Cyfyng, on the eastern edge of Capel Curig. Cross the narrow stone bridge and fork right up a broad farm lane. Follow this up the hill through gates to the point where it levels out before swinging left to the lake which Siabod hugs under its southern precipices.

Start at Pont Cyfyng GR 736571 Parking in loop of old road

The east ridge heads up uncompromisingly from here to the top. But you have a choice of plodding up grass slopes on the right or entertaining yourself on the rocky crest of the ridge. The horseshoe walk on Moel Siabod, ascending by the even-rockier south ridge, is of course a popular short day.

Moel Siabod 872m 4km from road

From the summit you have to swing almost due west at first. The descent is over steep grass, with the Glyders directly in front of you. Go left over a

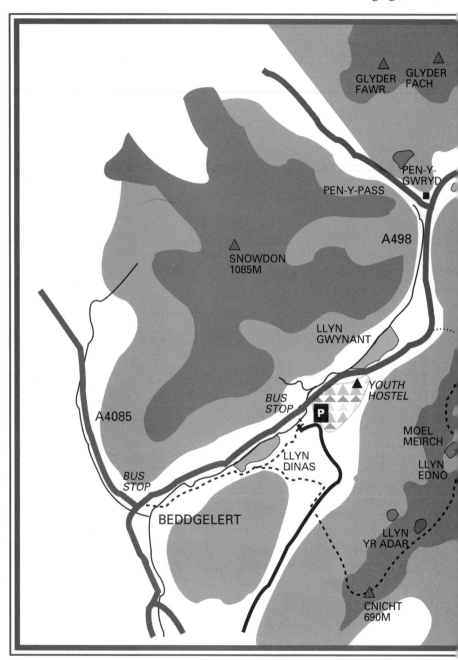

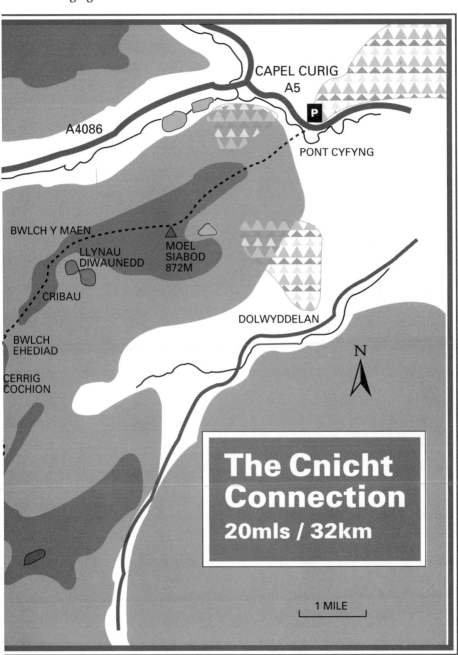

CAPEL CURIG
A5

P

PONT CYFYNG

A4086

BWLCH Y MAEN

LLYNAU
DIWAUNEDD

MOEL
SIABOD
872M

CRIBAU

DOLWYDDELAN

BWLCH
EHEDIAD

N

CERRIG
COCHION

The Cnicht
Connection
20mls / 32km

1 MILE

ladder stile and along a wide grassy ridge to
Bwlch-y-Maen.

Now the bones of the landscape are starting to
show through. The path gets rockier and more
playful. Circle round the head of a small cwm
containing the twin lakes of Llysau Diwaunedd.
Occasionally, iron stakes appear, marking a dis-   *Follow boundary*
trict boundary. They are as good a guide as any   *markers*
over the twisted ground.

You can't mistake Bwlch Ehediadd. A wide
watery trench confronts you, and it will take all
your ingenuity to cross with dry feet. Try down to
the left.

Back up on to rock and heather you go, over   *Moel Meirch 609m*
Cerrig Cochion and Moel Meirch. A secluded
pocket of water lies below you, Llyn Edno. It's a
delightful spot to longer on a hot summer day,
and I have to admit that I have stayed too long
here on more than one occasion, and had to
scamper down to the road hurriedly to catch the
bus.

You have to gain the ridge on the far side of the   *Keep following the*
lake, Ysgafell Wen. The shortest route might   *boundary markers*
prove to be very wet, so it could be advisable to
circle round the western edge of the lake. More
tiny lakes appear beneath you, cradled in rocky
hollows. Keep an eye open for the boundary
markers.

Now the ground is flattening out and becoming
grassy again. Watch out for tiny hidden fissures
that can swallow your leg up to the knee. I always
seem to find one when I go along this section. But
don't worry if you get muddy shoes or boots.
They will get washed clean before you get to

Cnicht, whose gentle north ridge you can see in front.

Yes, it's paddling time again. If your mummy never let you do it with your shoes on, now's the time to indulge yourself. It's particularly squelchy without being muddy down by Llyn-yr-Adar.

Wet, wet, wet

You're probably more used to scaling Cnicht at the sharp end. Coming through the back door, there's hardly any uphill work. You join the well worn path of the Cwm Croesor circuit, and suddenly find yourself at the prow of the hill, probably meeting the first people since you left Siabod.

Cnicht 690m

The view over Tremadoc Bay will tempt you to stay a while. But you have a bus to catch, and a couple of hours of walking still to do.

Slither down scree ledges and slabs on the right-hand side of the sharp Cnicht nose. At the end of this steep drop, a gully slopes down to the right. Turn down the gully and head for a distant path alongside a stream. This will take you to a lane at Gelli-lago cottage.

Right at GR 644465

GR 632484

Turn right along the lane and left at the second cottage on a signposted path. Follow this over a rise and across a track to Hafod Owen. The little house is buried in a forest of rhododendrons. They may be a foreign weed on Welsh hillsides, but they make a brave show in late May.

Right for 700m along lane, then left

Your route descends through a sparse wood to the side of Llyn Dinas. The last bus for Capel Curig leaves Beddgelert at four thirty, so if time is tight, turn right to pick it up by the Watkin Path

Get current timetable from Tourist Offices

car park. Otherwise, finish the walk with a stroll to Beddgelert and its cafés.

The Cnicht Connection is one of the shortest walks in the guide, but it is also one of the most enjoyable, so don't rush it. However, the necessarily early finish does make the route more challenging than you might expect. Give yourself time to enjoy the walk by starting early.

Cadair Idris from just below Llyn Cau (photo: Graham Beech)

CRAIGS OF CADAIR

End-to-end on Idris

22 mls/35km   8 hrs
Ascent: 3,750ft/1,145m

Cadair Idris stands proudly apart from the other major summits of North Wales. It claims all the long line of precipices which wall in the southern side of the beautiful Mawddach estuary. Ninety nine percent of ascents are made direct to the central top, by the route replacing the discredited Foxes Path, or by the preferable south ridge. Neither of these approaches takes advantage of the nine mile long ridge which is so impressive viewed across the estuary. This walk does.

OS Landranger Map 124

The starting point is conventional, the car park near Llyn Gwernan. But coming on to the road, you will turn left whilst everyone else will turn right to join the easy footpath to the top.

Start at GR 698154 Car Park Kings Youth Hostel 2km

I'm going to ask you to walk along the road to start the day. It's far from wearisome, with the lake on your left and views to the heart of the estuary opening up. Twenty five minutes will take you to a right turn at Rhyd Wen farm, up a very narrow lane. It soon abandons its stone walls, crossing open pasture and curving through birch woods to a T-junction just over a river bridge.

2km 500m on road Direct path from hostel 2km 500m to bridge

Turn right again. Your feet won't be on tarmac for much longer. When the lane finally swings right into a farm gate marked 'private' walk straight

Turn right 1km to lane-head

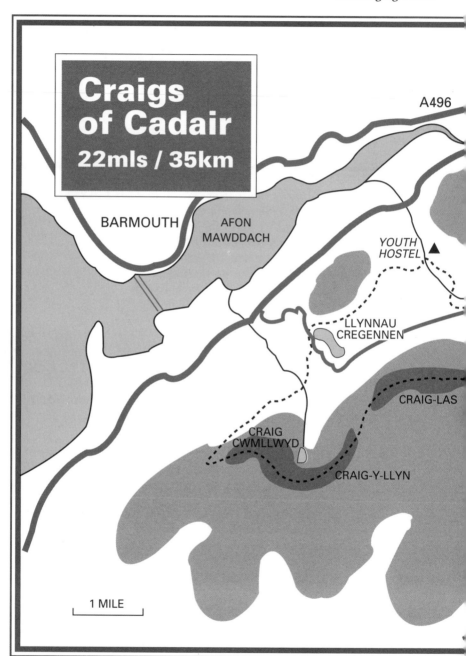

**Craigs
of Cadair**
22mls / 35km

A496

BARMOUTH

AFON
MAWDDACH

YOUTH
HOSTEL

LLYNNAU
CREGENNEN

CRAIG-LAS

CRAIG
CWMLLWYD

CRAIG-Y-LLYN

1 MILE

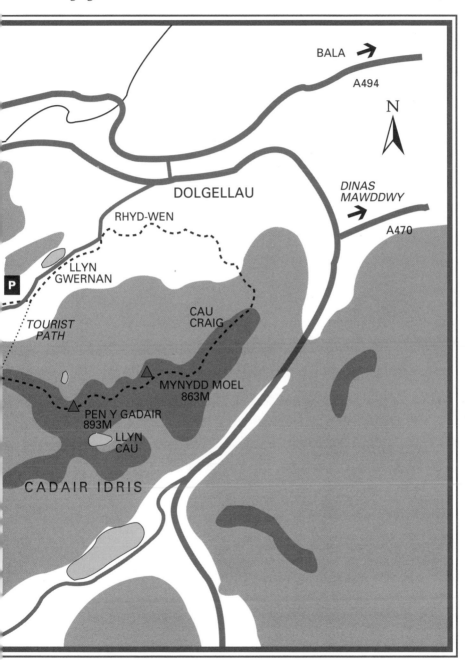

on, as indicated by a footpath sign in Welsh. Keep alongside the wall until a homemade sign sends you left across the field to a defined track. Turn right up this towards the ridge. As you climb, disregard a ladder stile over a fence to the right but stay in sight of the fence for the best trail up towards an obvious dip in the skyline.

Follow sign

When you gain the ridge, a panorama over central Wales opens up before you. I always find it difficult to identify individual hills, but perhaps you know them better than I do. A ladder stile crosses a wall in front. Don't cross it. Turn right instead up the short rocky slope of Cau Craig that will take you in only a quarter of an hour to a wide and, yes, marshy ridge.

Turn right on ridge to Cau Craig

In front, you can see the final climb to the summit. Well, that's what it looks like, but in fact it is the subsidiary top of Mynydd Moel. It's only a hundred feet lower then Pen-y-gader, so most of the day's climbing really is over early.

Mynydd Moel 863m Pen-y-Gader 893m/2927ft

Whilst you are resting on the summit and enjoying the view, I must tell you a story about a friend's experience up here. We'll call him a mature member of the Rucksack Club. Occasionally he likes to camp high, away from busy valley sites. A couple of years ago, he took his tent up Cadair Idris, accompanied only by a flask of his favourite Scotch.

Have you heard this one?

He was in a deep sleep, perhaps dreaming happily of discovering a Munro unknown to anyone else, when he was rudely brought back to wakefulness by the ministrations of a mountain rescue team. Apparently, some tidy-minded people, unable to comprehend that someone would camp on a summit by choice, had jumped to the conclusion that my friend was in some sort of trouble, and had called in the mountain rescue. I wish I could have heard what he said to his would-be rescuers!

From the summit, a broad cairned track leads down the west ridge, the main path from your car park. You'll get the most impressive views of Cadair's northern precipices if you keep to the crest. My visit for the guide coincided with the Cadair Fell Race. I paused where the track turns sharply downhill, to watch the runners gasp upwards. There's a guilty pleasure in seeing other people suffer!

Our route goes straight on, over Craig-las, on grassland now. Keep on going, close to a fence, and descend to a saddle. In front, a hill cwm holds a small lake. Yes, you do have to climb again round its head, over Craig-y-Llyn. *Craig-las*

Two thirds of the way round, when you are descending the other side of Craig-y-Llyn, keep to the right of the fence, although you will see stiles inside fields on the left. Sweep round to the right by a plantation to the top of Craig cwm Llwyd then turn down a grassy slope to a stony track crossing the ridge from the left. *Craig-y-Llyn*

Craig cwm Llwyd

You are almost opposite the railway bridge to Barmouth. Turn back east along the track. The easy walking will allow you to enjoy the views across the estuary to the Rhinogs. Fork right along a track marked on my old map as Ffordd Ddu, to a stream crossing and a gate. *Turn right on track*

A footpath goes from here, cutting off the corner to the lakes of Llynau Cregennen, but I have to confess I missed it in my haste. It does emerge near the western end of the lakes. If you want a *GR 648134* spot to linger, to absorb your day, have a drink, take some photographs, this is it.

Turn left along the shore lane. At the top of a very short hill, where the road bends left, follow a sign on the right, over a ladder stile, and along the northern shore. At the further end of the lake, where the arrows try to send you round in a complete circuit, go straight on along a broad trail through the heather.

Circle northern shore

Yellow arrows

From here, you get the best views of the day of Cadair's northern precipices, so save some film. It seems a little unfair that such a worthy mountain should not attain the dignity of a three-thousander. On the other hand, it would have made it awkward to fit all the three-thousander peaks into one day.

The trail crosses a field and joins a narrow lane. Follow this past a ruined church, down through woodland to Kings Youth Hostel. Turn right in front of the hostel, over a river bridge, then right again through a camping field. Keep the river on your right up through woods. Bear right over a feeder stream, past a farm, to the road. The car park is a few minutes walk to left. Just before you reach it, Ty Nant offers teas.

Turn right at hostel

BOWLAND DOUBLE

The answer to access

30mls/48km   10 hrs
Ascent: 4,000ft/1,220m

As we speed north to the Lakes on the motorway, most of us cast a glance at the line of attractive hills to the right. But the Forest of Bowland is notorious for restrictions on access. There are just a couple of very small areas on the western slopes where walkers are allowed to wander freely, a concession path along part of the highest ridge, and a few linear routes that appear to have no return links. So we shrug our shoulders and drive on.

That has been my attitude too. Until this guide-book gave me the incentive to search the Bowland Hills for a worthwhile walking route. The key that unlocked the door proved to be distance. A satisfying circuit of what might be called a normal day length of about fifteen miles is still difficult to find. But twice that distance enables you to make a double crossing of the best part of the Bowland Fells.

OS Landranger Maps 97, 102 plus 103 for Slaidburn Ranger Office 0995 61693

I planned the route on my only map of the area, an old Bartholomew's half inch edition. It showed a long straight line of dots crossing Salter Fell, north of Slaidburn. I knew about a limited access path to Ward's Stone, highest point in Bowland. I decided to try to connect these up.

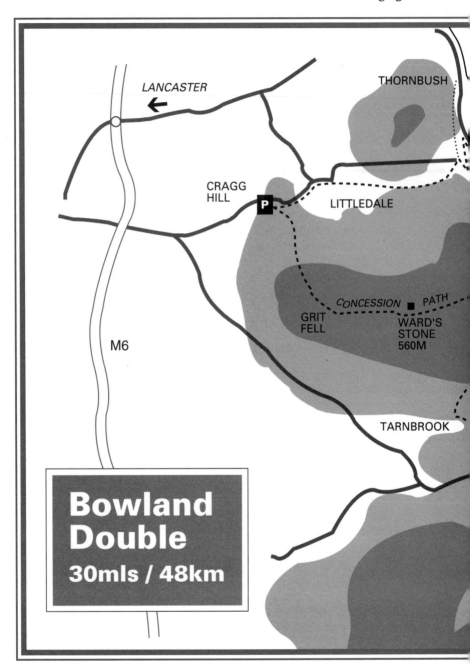

LANCASTER

THORNBUSH

CRAGG HILL

LITTLEDALE

P

CONCESSION ■ PATH

GRIT FELL

WARD'S STONE 560M

M6

TARNBROOK

Bowland Double

30mls / 48km

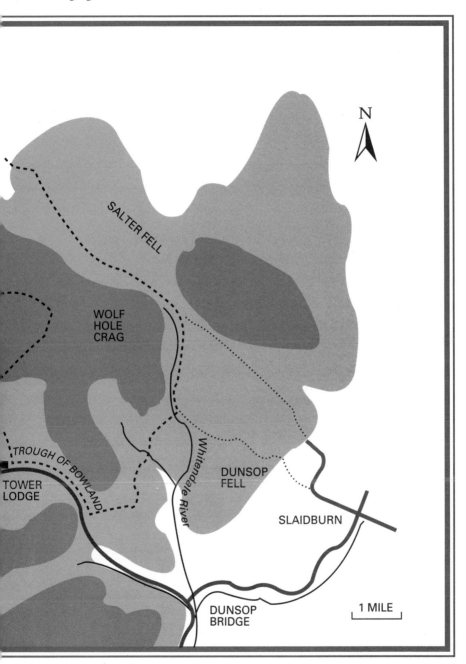

For my pioneering trip, I started at the southern end of the Salter Fell crossing. It's a seven mile long hill pass reminiscent of Scotland, bordered by breezy slopes alive with plovers and curlews. Unfortunately, there are only a few awkward places to park a car on the verge of the approach lane. I therefore recommend you start at Cragg Hill, east of Lancaster, where there is a parking area. This starting point also has the advantage of putting the hardest work at the beginning of the day.

Start at Cragg Hill
GR 547617
Car park

Anyone staying at Slaidburn Youth Hostel, however, could use this southern approach. The distance would be increased to around thirty eight miles, making it quite a hard day.

Alternative start at Slaidburn

The parking area at Cragg Hill is on top of a sharp little ascent. Just walk across the road on the brow of the hill to start the walk.

The way across two fields and round a barn is well marked. Turn right round the corner of a wall and you arrive at a ladder stile at the boundary of the open access area.

Yellow arrows

A sign immediately beyond the stile defines the limits in red: a square at the western end of the ridge and a thin finger stretching out beyond Ward's Stone before cutting down abruptly to the Tarnbrook Valley.

Open access

Go straight up the hillside behind the sign to gain a path which cuts diagonally left-wards through the heather towards the skyline. On top, the path is more defined as it climbs steadily towards Ward's Stone. If you're used to Peak District outcrops, you won't find this modest heap very impressive, but it does mark the topmost point of

Ward's Stone 1836ft

the Bowland hills. And if the day is clear, the view is certainly impressive, particularly across Morecambe Bay to the Cumbrian hills.

Beyond, there's no wide trail to follow. Most people making the ascent return by the same route, as the concession path in front drops into the valley of the River Wyre, a long lane-walk from the start.

Concession path, occasional posts

Wooden posts with splashes of faded paint mark the permitted route, but they are few and far between. Soon you reach a fence along the ridge, and the ground gets much wetter. I managed to keep my feet dry to this point – remember I started near Slaidburn – so I was annoyed when a leg plunged into mud when I was crossing a slimy ditch.

When the fence meets a stone wall, bear right along the southern side of the wall, and keep going along another fence which in turn replaces the wall. Everyone who walks on the ridge remarks upon the seagulls, but I wasn't prepared for their extravagant number. It was like a scene from the famous Hitchcock film, and the screaming was incessant.

Beware low flying gulls

I expected the valley-wards turn of the concession path to be very positively marked. But, distracted by the gulls and attempts to find the driest line, I followed a line of bootprints too far towards Wolf Hole Crag. I don't think it would have made any difference if I had been using a large scale map rather than my faithful Barts half inch because the terrain up there is much of a muchness.

Turn right opposite ladder stile

You should look for a ladder stile over the fence on the left. You have to turn right there of course, and almost immediately you are on to a more defined path, marked by posts at frequent intervals. The path descends gently to a steam, crosses it above a miniature waterfall, then joins a wide track that goes all the way down into the valley.

I have never heard or seen so many curlews as I did on Tarnbrook Fell that June day. Maybe it's because they can breed undisturbed by crowds of walkers. Are there some advantages to restricted access after all?

Twitchers' paradise

Having said that, it's a pity the concession path doesn't extend all the way along the ridge to the Trough of Bowland. It would save two climbs on the circuit. But on the other hand, the valleys could be said to be the most attractive parts of Bowland.

In the valley, the track from Tarnbrook Fell goes along a wall to the edge of the access area. By the access sign, a twin of the one near the start of the walk, follow a footpath arrow left towards a farm. The path takes you past the buildings and over a low hillside. Dropping down the other side, you cross a ladder stile, descend two fields to a wide track, and emerge on the Trough of Bowland road at Tower Lodge.

Yellow arrows

The walk over the Trough is probably the prettiest part of the route. Most of the way the road is fringed by what must be called a greensward, dotted with pines. Unfortunately, the crossing of the pass is a popular Sunday excursion for everyone in the north-west who owns wheels. So you'll have to share the road with cars, motorbikes and pedal cycles. But it's only two and a half miles. The scenery is delightful. And if all those vehicles manage to avoid the ducks wander-

Trough of Bowland

ing about in the road outside Tower Lodge, there's a fair chance they will miss you too.

4km on road

On the eastern side of the pass, the road dives down steeply. As it starts to level out, there is a barn on the left, the first building on the descent. A gate at the side of the barn opens on to a track. This important link path is not signposted.

Turn left at barn

The track swings up round a wood, past a ruined farm, and over open hillside to a ladder stile. Above the stile, keep to the left-hand side of a gully to the top of the ridge. On the eastern side of the hill, the slope is steeper, and the path cuts a diagonal line down to the fields of Brennand Farm.

Cross ridge

Go left at the farm, through two gates, and follow the farm track round a sharp right-hand bend. Turn left on another track up the hillside, then right at a signposted stile alongside a wall. You are crossing a neck of hill to the Whitendale river valley. On top, there's an oily marsh which is unavoidable – unless you choose to walk all the way round Brennand Knoll and back up by the River Whitendale on a good dry track. It probably wouldn't take all that much longer, and it's certainly prettier.

Turn left in farm, round bend, over saddle

If you started at Slaidburn you have to turn right when you reach the valley, to cross Dunsop Fell. The main route turns left, towards the source of the river. On each side, the fells close in. The long hillside in front is Salter Fell. From this low angle, you can't see the wide shelf track which runs along it.

Right for Slaidburn, left for Cragg Hill

When you're up on to it, the Salter Fell trail offers a highway back to the north side of the Bowland

Left along major trail for 6km

hills. Parts of it are a little ugly underfoot, where gullies have been filled in with old car tyres, presumably to facilitate the passage of four wheel drive vehicles. But the surrounding fells have a fresh clean look which I suppose is the result of their being managed for grouse shooting.

Seven miles after leaving the road-head on the southern side of the hills, the Salter Fell track becomes a lane again. On your circuit, you joined it halfway of course.

Higher, Mid and Lower Salter farms

After a mile on the lane, just beyond Mid Salter farm, you have a choice. You can carry on along the lane for another mile to a left turn on to a farm road at Thornbush. Or, more interestingly, you can turn left at the footpath sign, across a meadow, down to a sheltered picnic spot by the River Roeburn.

Left at sign

Cross stream, up hill, right by wall

If you take this route, follow a farm road across the river, up a hill through two gates. Just short of a farm you have another choice. An ill-defined right of way goes straight past the farm. It's preferable to turn right along another farm access road, down a dip, and up the other side to meet the farm road from Thornbush, near Winder Farm. Turn left to a signpost pointing through a gate to Deep Clough and Littledale Hall.

Left at path T-junction

Fork left on path

Am I giving you too many alternatives? There's now a fourth. The footpath along the valley takes you into the tiny hamlet of Crossgill. If you're interested in architecture, there's an unusually good example of a stone building conversion on the right. You can get to the same spot by walking along the lane above, from where you get better views. Go through Crossgill, turn left at the next crossroads, down a hill, up a twisting ascent, and you are back at the parking place on Cragg Hill.

Or keep to the lane and turn left

Left at crossroads for 1km 500m

GATES OF EDEN

A taste of the northern Pennines

27mls/43km   9 hrs

Ascent: 3,600ft/1,100m

Much of the northern Pennines is most easily accessible from the east, and is therefore outside the scope of this guide. An exception is the Eden valley. It's only a quarter of an hour's drive from Junction 38 on the M6 to Kirkby Stephen, a pleasant market town surrounded by hill walking opportunities. The circuit I am suggesting takes you over Nine Standards Rigg, Mallerstang Edge and Wild Boar Fell in one moderately easy day. En route, you'll be able to inspect seventeen stone men lined up at attention on the high points for who-knows-how-long.

OS Landranger Maps 91 & 98

If you want to make the day a bit more of a challenge, take inspiration from the distance, which is around race marathon length. Almost all of the route is runnable, and there's a café just over half way round, so you won't need to carry much food. Six hours would be a reasonable target time for a fell run, as opposed to nine hours for steady walking.

Hill Marathon opportunity

Kirkby Stephen is on the Wainwright coast-to-coast walk of course. For the first hour or so you will be following this popular route through the hamlet of Hartley up to Nine Standards Rigg. There are paths from the town centre for part of the way to Hartley, but the lane leading off to the right just north of the market square gives you a more straightforward start to a long day.

Start at Kirkby Stephen GR 775087 Sunday parking in market place

At the outskirts of Hartley, turn right past the houses. The lane climbs up by the side of a large quarry and round the shoulder of the hill. It loses its surface where a bridleway signpost points left alongside a stone wall. A metal sign on a gate reassures you that you are on the coast-to-coast route. Another sign on the next gate asks you to follow the permissive path to Nine Standards, because of erosion problems.

Lane to Hartley
Right at T-junction
Fork left at far end of lane on to bridleway

You are almost at the top of the hill before you come upon the permissive path, signed as being the direct route to Nine Standards, and looking more eroded than the bridleway. It takes you past a small cairn newly built in the style of the nine stone men which soon line up against the sky. Their grouping seems to be haphazard, so perhaps they were built individually, at different times, to commemorate people or events. Whatever their original purpose, they make a striking foreground for photographs of otherwise featureless fells.

Fork left on permissive path

Stone men

The top of the hill is over to the right, marked by both a trig point and an orientation table. Aim your eye along the lines pointing towards High Seat and Hugh Seat, and you'll see a path heading in that direction. The coast-to-coast route continues along the ridge to the left.

Nine Standards Rigg

Orientation table - head for High Seat

Unfortunately, the path soon gets sucked into the maw of Rollinson Haggs, but you eventually emerge on to a track coming down from the left. You could probably join this track higher up by going beyond the trig point, but it wouldn't be so much fun as hurdling ooze-filled channels.

Nice bit of bog

Turn right down the track. It appears to be taking you back to Kirkby, but by a prominent pile of

Right down track, left at stones

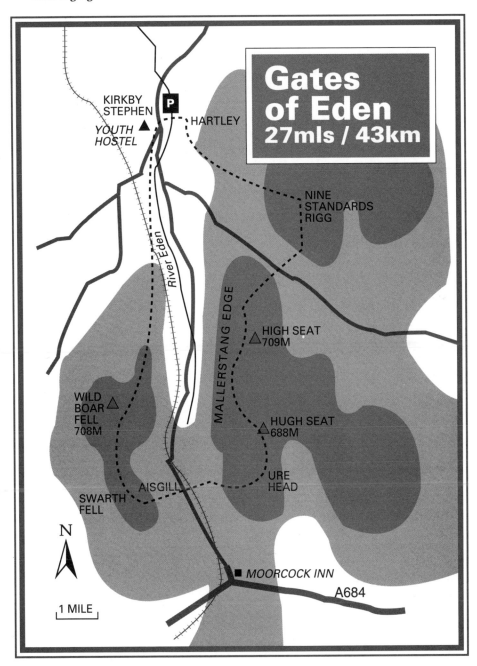

Gates
of Eden
27mls / 43km

KIRKBY
STEPHEN
YOUTH
HOSTEL

HARTLEY

NINE
STANDARDS
RIGG

River Eden

MALLERSTANG EDGE

HIGH SEAT
709M

WILD
BOAR
FELL
708M

HUGH SEAT
688M

URE
HEAD

AISGILL

SWARTH
FELL

N

MOORCOCK INN
A684

1 MILE

stones, a path curls down to the left, heading for
the high point of the road to Keld. In front, you
will probably see the brightly coloured canopies
of hang gliders swooping over Tailbridge Hill.

Swing left across a stream, and you will realise *Nateby Common*
you are on limestone, with dry turf underfoot for *Cross road to High*
a change. Enjoy it while you can. When you cross *Pike Hill*
the road and head up High Pike Hill, you're back
on to the bogs. The easiest way goes up on the
left, on a fairly well defined track.

Once you're on top, it's easy going along an
occasionally cairned narrow path in the centre of
what is almost a plateau. There's hardly any rise *High Seat*
to High Seat, highest point on this side of the *709m/2328ft*
Eden Valley.

You haven't been seeing much of the view to the
west, across to Wild Boar Fell. So I suggest that *Fork right at large*
instead of carrying on along the ridge to Hugh *cairn*
Seat (very confusing those two names) you now
swing towards Mallerstang Edge. A few minutes
across flat moorland will take you to the top of
the edge. There are good views back north along *Follow edge past*
the broken rocks. Follow the path above Hanging *stone figures*
Stone Scar, past what should perhaps be called
stone children, identical triplets much smaller
than their Nine Standards parents, staring across
the valley at their cousins on Wild Boar Fell.

Keep on top of the tongue of hill as it heads
directly for the cottages at Aisgill Moor. There's
not much in the way of a path until you're nearly *Hell Gill bridge*
at Hell Gill. The medieval High Way comes in
from the right, and takes you to a bridge over the
gill. You don't want to cross the bridge, but do
take time to peer over its walls down into the
surprisingly deep and narrow gorge it spans.

Go through the gate just before the bridge, down a track, and across the Settle-Carlisle railway line to Aisgill Moor Cottages. The tea room here welcomes walkers and cyclists. I can't imagine anyone missing the opportunity to sneak at least a cuppa before tackling the last big climb of the day.

Turn right before bridge

Café

A footpath sign almost opposite the café points to Grisedale, but you have to head straight up the hillside, roughly following the county boundary. Gain the skyline at Swarth Fell Pike, and follow the ridge to the Swarth Fell cairn at the northwest end.

Cross road

Swarth Fell 681m/2235ft

Ahead, there's a short descent to a saddle, and beyond, the bulk of Wild Boar Fell. It always seems to wear a cap of cloud when I'm there. It did so when I checked the route for the guide, yet irritatingly there were clear skies to the south over Three Peaks country. As I started the ascent from the saddle, the cloud settled even lower, and covered the whole fell.

Drop to saddle and small tarn

The path follows a fence at first, then veers right to the sharp edge on the eastern side of Wild Boar Fell. Stone figures on High White Scar loomed eerily out of the mist. According to a guidebook, there are five. I'm sure there were more, grouped menacingly round me on that grey afternoon, but I didn't stop to count them. I hurriedly hopped over the fence and fled along the path on the edge of the escarpment.

Wild Boar Fell 708m/2324ft

More stone men

There's a dip and short rise before you finally descend to the lower moorlands. Where the path divides, keep to the left, along the top of the ridge. As the ground flattens out, you reach an unfenced lane. Cross this and head along an in-

Left at fork

Cross lane

creasingly defined track towards a wide green
lane funnelled between stone walls.

Follow green lane

You can now see the railway line on your right.
Ignore a tunnel under the line, and keep going   *Right over bridge*
along the green lane to a bridge. Turn right over
the railway line and down a track to another
surfaced lane.

Left on lane

Turn left to one of those old red telephone boxes,   *Right at 'phone box*
where a sign points right down a bridleway to   *to Wharton Hall*
Wharton Hall. At first it's bounded by stone
walls, then it crosses fields. Turn right through a
gate along a concrete farm road down to the Hall.

Modern farm buildings look a little out of place
against the weathered stone walls of the Hall. The
elegantly   proportioned   seventeenth   century
manor house has been built on the ruins of an
earlier fortified dwelling. A massive gateway,
down to the right, is worthy of a castle.

The farm road takes you straight to the outskirts
of Kirkby, but there's a mile of houses before you
reach the market place.

ONE-WAY TICKET

The best alternative to the Three Peaks walk?

25mls/40km   9 hours
Ascent: 3,500ft/1,065m

You probably know the Yorkshire Three Peaks area better than I do. Certainly the writers of the many Dales guide books must have tramped every path, way and lane. So it would be presumptuous of me to think I could devise an original route. Wouldn't it?

OS Landranger Map 98

As the name implies, the key to my route is an initial journey by train from Settle to Dent, over the famous Ribblehead viaduct no less. There are special ramblers' excursions of course, linked to guided walks, but these don't exploit the full advantage of the train. Look at the map and you will see that going by rail from Settle up the Ribble Valley to Dent station places you in a position to traverse both Whernside and Ingleborough on your walk back, without getting too involved with the Three Peaks circuit. You might also realise that the route finishes through an interesting triangle of landscape north west of Settle. This was certainly new to me. I was delighted to discover stone walled bridleways massed with Crane's-bill and Meadowsweet in full summer bloom.

Start at Settle station GR 817634, Limited parking at station, town carparks nearby. Train about 9.45 in 1993 timetable.

But let's get you off on that train. It's unlikely to be a steam special, but twenty five minutes or so will see you at Dent station. En route, you cross the Ribblehead viaduct, but I have to warn you not to get too excited at the thought. You might

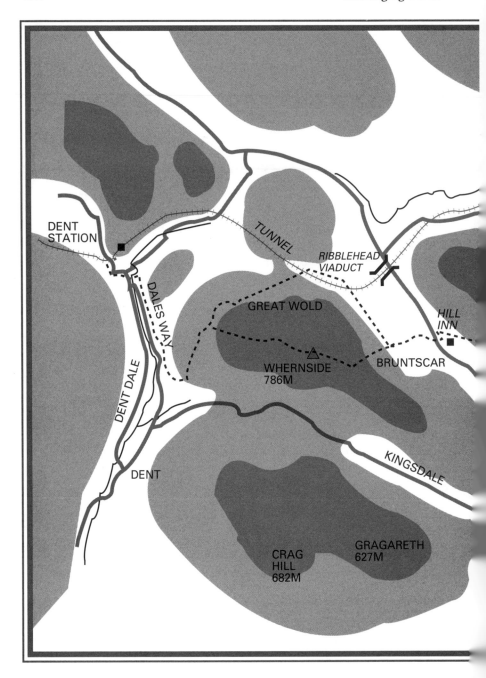

DENT
STATION

TUNNEL

RIBBLEHEAD
VIADUCT

GREAT WOLD

DALES WAY

DENT DALE

HILL
INN

WHERNSIDE
786M

BRUNTSCAR

DENT

KINGSDALE

CRAG
HILL
682M

GRAGARETH
627M

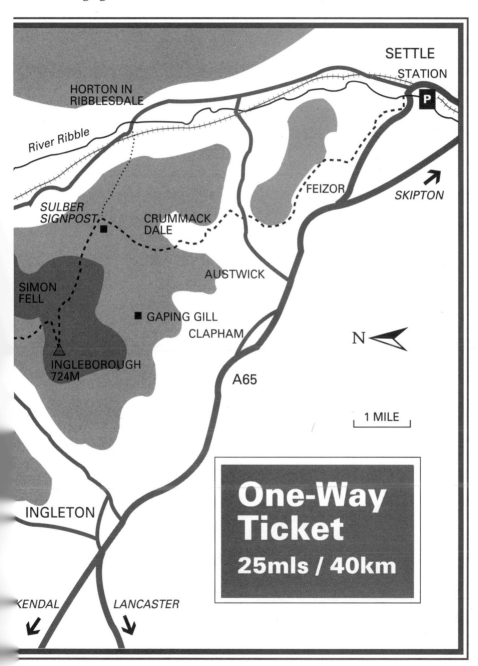

SETTLE

STATION

HORTON IN
RIBBLESDALE

P

River Ribble

FEIZOR

SKIPTON

SULBER
SIGNPOST

CRUMMACK
DALE

AUSTWICK

SIMON
FELL

GAPING GILL

CLAPHAM

N

INGLEBOROUGH
724M

A65

1 MILE

One-Way
Ticket
25mls / 40km

INGLETON

KENDAL

LANCASTER

just as well be on a not-so-high bank. There's no feeling of being poised above the valley.

Dent station is, of course, nowhere near Dent village, but perched up on the hillside at the head of the dale. Walk downhill and turn left at the T-junction. Cross a stone bridge over the River Dee, then turn immediately right on to a slim path along the side of the river. You're back on to a lane in a quarter of a mile, and the same distance will take you to a gate on the left. The path that leads off across a meadow is part of the Dales Way, but is not signposted as such. It takes you through two belts of conifers, across a farm track, to an unsurfaced lane. Frankly, you'll probably find it pleasanter to walk along the valley lane, where you're not bothered with a 'Beware of the Bull' notice.

Start walking downhill.

Left over bridge, right along path.

Straight on along lane for 500m or 1500m

Ingleborough from near the Hill Inn

Turn left up the farm lane and follow it round to the right. Opposite a house, a stile starts a sequence of field paths that emerge on to yet another farm track. There is a Dales Way sign now, but your route is to the left, on a path which circles round the back of a farm and on to much rougher pasture. When you are clear of the walls, swing left up the hill to a gate. Here, you can see a stile over a skyline wall. Yellow-topped posts firmly shepherd you round the shoulder of the hill to a wall and signpost. On the further side of the wall, you're on the Craven Way, although my map calls it the Dales Way.

Left on farm lane, right over stile.

Left at sign. Bear left beyond farm.

Left after sign at GR 729854

It's a wide scar of a track which climbs steadily over Great Wold, the northern spread of Whernside. Two finger cairns are prominent on the ridge line. The track soon gains the dignity of a wall on both sides. After a gate, you can think about turning south up the two-mile-long spine of Whernside. Head well to the left of the cairns and you will pass close to a couple of tarns before you gain the summit wall. Keep to the western side of the wall and you will stay on grass. Hop back to the eastern side at the summit trig point.

Turn right after gate

Whernside 736m

You can see Ingleborough now, not too far distant. The much-used track which descends to the valley could be a lot worse. I hate the steps that have been built to minimise erosion. Stones laid with a natural tilt would look better and be easier to walk on.

You leave your first summit behind at a gate, and turn left along a farm road, directed by a Hill Inn signpost. Go left to the pub at the valley road. You should reach here conveniently close to lunch time.

Hill Inn for liquid lunch?

Just beyond the inn, a stone stile gives access to a   *Right after pub. 4km*
path cutting across to the main Ingleborough   *to the top*
ascent track. Turn right when you join it and
follow it round through fields to the start of a
broad walk which snakes to the foot of the final
steep pitch. It's made of hinged wooden sections
whose surface has been tarred and gritted. Unfortunately, plastic bags which contained the
material have been left on the hillside.

Whatever you think of prepared paths, the one up
Ingleborough certainly gets you easily up the hill.
At a sharp change of angle, boards give way to
rock and high semi-natural steps which must
have slimmed a few thighs.

On my route-resolving walk, I was tempted to
carry on straight to Settle from the saddle, as the
summit of Ingleborough is not exactly unfamiliar.
But I do try to do the complete walks, so I turned
right instead.
                                                        Ingleborough 724m

At the top I was rewarded with a quick flash of a
cheeky smile from an attractive young woman,
who I think was on the last lap of the Three Peaks
circuit. It made me regret that I was heading for
Settle rather than Horton. I hope you appreciate
the sacrifices I make for you. Who knows what
might have come of a companiable mug of tea at
the Pen y Ghent café?
                                                        Return to saddle

It's surprisingly far from the top of Ingleborough
to Settle – nine miles as the crow flies and even
further for walkers and magpies. So you are little
more than half way in distance, although all the
hill climbing effort is behind you. Head down the
descent path under Simon Fell towards Horton.   *Fork left*
Just after a ruined hut there's a gate in a wall,
followed by a fork in the trail. The right hand

branch cuts off a corner, but it's more interesting
to carry on across the limestone to that lonely   GR777735
signpost at Sulber.

Turn right on the grassy bridleway and follow it   *Right at 'BW*
to an obvious fork at a small cairn. Take the left *Clapham'*
hand trail, and it will lead you down into Crummack Dale, with good views of the limestone cliffs
girding the valley. Join a farm road, and take the *Left in 800m 'BW*
first lane on the left.   *Wharfe'*

This is the start of those stone walled bridleways I
found so pleasing. Just after a stone-flag foot-
bridge across a stream, the walls of the lane
squeeze closer together. Waist high grasses and
flowers hem the narrow path. You would need to
plunge into them if a horse came along.

You pop out of the end of this first section of
bridleway at Wharfe, a pristine hamlet. Turn left *Turn left, bear right.*
and swing immediately right to a surfaced lane.   *Right on road.*
Go right here, and take the first walled trail on   *Left in 150m.*
the left past Wood End farm. After a corner, the   *Left at crossroads.*
trail narrows again as far as a crossroads. Turn
sharp left, still on those walled bridleways.

At a ruined barn, take the left-hand fork, on a   *Fork left.*
path held even more tightly between the walls, to *Left, right at 'FP*
Feizor. Go left and almost immediately right, this *Stackhouse'*
time on a bridleway across open pasture. Near the
crest of a rise, fork right through a couple of   *Fork right at*
fields, to the top of Giggleswick Scar.   *Bridleway sign*

You're close to a main road now, but so high
above it you're not aware of the traffic. As you
start to drop (geographically not physically) turn *Left through gate,*
left through a gate in a stone wall, signposted   *sign Giggleswick*
Giggleswick. The path traverses between two tiers
of limestone, then drops steeply into a grassy

bowl. Turn left on to a wide trail down through a   *Left through gate into*
wood. This takes you on to a valley lane, past a   *wood*
house. However, looking at the map with a magnifying glass after the walk, I see that the dotted
red line of the right of way swings up behind the
house and goes directly to the main road. There
are only a few paces, however, which may or may
not be legal, on the shortest route.

The valley lane meets the main road at a T-   *Left at main road*
junction. Turn left to Settle town centre. There is a
narrow cut-through from the high railway bridge
straight to the station.

Reliving the walk as I wrote up the description,
the conviction grew on me that it was preferable
to the famous Three Peaks circuit. True, it doesn't
include Pen y Ghent, but neither does it include
those boring, boggy miles from Pen y Ghent to
Ribblehead. One-way Ticket is about the same
length, but offers a greater variety of landscape
and high quality walking throughout.

The only drawback is that the route doesn't finish
at the welcoming Pen y Ghent café in Horton. I
can remember rewarding myself with a magnificent breakfast there, after a December Three Peaks
walk. But you could try a second, shorter version
in the winter, picking up the train at Horton,
couldn't you?

LANGDALE HORSESHOE

The stony heart of Lakeland

18mls/29km   9 hrs

Ascent: 6,000ft/1,830m

Yes, I know. This is far from being an original route. But I am including it for the same reasons that make it a classic Lakeland horseshoe. It is a continuously interesting high level circuit of modest length in the most easily accessible part of the Lakes. Moreover, it is an ideal choice for someone attempting a hard mountain circuit for the first time, as there are several escape paths to the valley.

OS English Lakes South West or Harveys Western Lakeland

I also get the opportunity to make another dedication. It's to all the people whose company I have enjoyed on Pete's Mucky Walks. I'd better explain. A number of eclectic individuals have formed the habit of meeting up every December for a moderately sociable walk, set up by Pete of course, and at that time of year usually muddy. Hence the name. I was going to link the dedication to an extended version of our 1992 walk, but Pete's wife threatened me with excommunication and no more tea and crumpets when I called if I brought your eager feet scurrying through their personal corner of Lakeland. However, the Langdale Horseshoe has been on the menu in the past, so it's just as appropriate.

The popular version of the circuit starts at the head of the valley and goes direct to Pike o'

Start at Elterwater GR 327047

Blisco, over Crinkle Crags, Bowfell and the Langdale Pikes, and drops down again from Stickle
Tarn to the New Dungeon Ghyll hotel. I'm sure
that readers of this guide will consider this walk
to be too short and easy. Starting further down
the valley at Elterwater adds an appetising first
course along Lingmoor, and a dessert of the
grassy ridge that tumbles along between Langdale
and Easedale.

Pay car park in
village
Free car park on
common

Walk past the youth hostel and take the first lane
on the right. Keep right past a cottage where an
unsurfaced road forks left, and follow the lane as
it climbs slightly. Just short of a second cottage,
fork left on to a bridleway. This mounts pleasantly through oak woods and an old quarry. Just
below the ridge the trail fades into the hillside,
and you have to turn sharply left, up a few
zigzags to gain the skyline.

First right, keep right.

800m from village
fork left on bridleway

Cross to the south side of a stone wall and turn
along the ridge, on a series of ascending dips, if
that doesn't sound a contradictory description.
When you reach the top point of Lingmoor Fell,
cross back over the wire fence that has replaced
the wall. This must be one of the best mid-height
viewpoints in the Lakes. Pike o' Blisco, Crinkle
Crags, Bowfell and the Langdale Pikes are
arrayed in a half circle in front of you. Their
skyline is your route for the day. Drop down to
the saddle before Side Pike, turn left to descend
again to the road, and turn right to the Pike o'
Blisco path.

Follow crest to
Lingmoor Fell top

Descend to dip, turn
left to road
Right on road

It's hardly necessary to describe the central part of
the route, the main course if we're maintaining
the menu metaphor. Your first ventures in fell
walking were probably on these hills. But, for the
record, the shortest route to Pike o' Blisco blazes

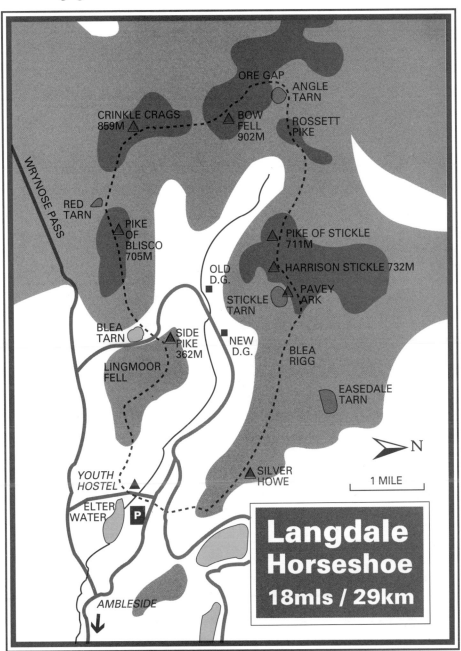

ORE GAP

ANGLE TARN

CRINKLE CRAGS 859M

BOW FELL 902M

ROSSETT PIKE

WRYNOSE PASS

RED TARN

PIKE OF BLISCO 705M

PIKE OF STICKLE 711M

HARRISON STICKLE 732M

OLD D.G.

STICKLE TARN

PAVEY ARK

BLEA TARN

SIDE PIKE 362M

NEW D.G.

BLEA RIGG

LINGMOOR FELL

EASEDALE TARN

N

YOUTH HOSTEL

ELTER WATER

P

SILVER HOWE

1 MILE

AMBLESIDE

Langdale Horseshoe
18mls / 29km

up to the right of the hump facing you, above the
beck, and gains the skyline between the Pike and
Blake Rigg.

The Langdale Pikes from Lingmoor Fell

Now is the time to mention a peculiar feature of the walk. Several sections turn out to be longer than you expect them to be, and the whole round of sixteen miles by the map certainly feels more like twenty. I've split the difference for the nominal length. The ascent of Pike o' Blisco is the first of these deceptive sections.

Pike o' Blisco/2304ft
705M

The easiest descent from the Pike to Red Tarn cuts back to the left. The path which continues over the shoulder of hillside leading to Crinkle Crags has been surfaced with rocks in an exemplary fashion, far better than those awkward steps on Whernside I mentioned in a previous route description.

Start counting

There are, so I'm told, five crinkles on Crinkle Crags, but the first is less pronounced, the main four standing close together like the knuckles on a clenched hand.

When I was repeating the route for the guide I overtook a distinguished old gentleman just before the first crinkle. Talking with his grand-daughter, who was further on, I discovered he was eighty three and had had four hip operations. I hope I will be able to do as much when I'm that old, and have a pretty girl to keep me company, too.

The direct route to the main cluster of crinkles goes up a short scree slope into a blind gully. Two high steps up a ten-feet-high wall on the right offer a way through. Dear old Alfred Wainwright twittered that this was 'quite beyond the power of the average walker to scale'. I wish he could have seen the gentleman's granddaughter climb straight up without a moment's hesitation.

If you don't like the short scramble, detour to the left.

I seem to be fated always to have cloud on Crinkle Crags. Even when I start in bright sunshine, under clear blue skies, grey vapours are whisked up from somewhere to obscure the view when I get to the top. Cloud wreathing round the rocks does add an air of mystery, but I'm sure you would prefer to see the views, so I'll promise to deny myself Crinkle Crags for a couple of years, to give you a better chance of completing the Langdale Horseshoe on a clear day.

Crinkle Crags
860m/2816ft

The path scrabbles over the stones of the crinkles and then becomes easier underfoot as it descends behind Shelter Crags to the grassy saddle at Three Tarns. It's a straight plod up scree to the top of Bowfell, highest summit on the route.

Bowfell 903m/
2960ft

On the northern side of Bowfell, the path slopes down to the left of the ridge, to Ore Gap. Don't get too obsessed with climbing every hill that confronts you, and forget to turn right here, down to Angle Tarn.

Right at GR 241072
Ore Gap

Angle Tarn

Cross the stream just below its exit from the tarn and start up the short slope leading to the Rossett Ghyll descent to Langdale. You can take the second path on the left and circle round the back of Rossett Pike or go higher and traverse the top. Either way you end up at Black Crags, and again you have the alternatives of climbing over the top or traversing below the cliffs, this time on the right-hand side on an occasionally-cairned thread of path. This section from Angle Tarn is another of those longer-than-you-think instances.

Rossett Pike

Black Crags

Join the well-used trail of the Stake Pass northwards to the first crest, then at a left-hand bend head straight up the hillside. The dramatic finger of Gimmer Crag is on the skyline. Just after the

Cross Stake
Pass trail

Pike of Stickle 2323ft

slope eases, you converge with a wide muddy trail that takes you over the back of the Langdale Pikes. If you have energy to spare, nip across to the craggy summits. By this time, though, you'll probably be happy to head straight for the top of Pavey Ark.

Harrison Stickle 736m 2403ft

You have another choice here, of scrambling down Jack's Rake, or following the cairned path that takes you down the back of Pavey Ark, and which keeps you conveniently above Stickle Tarn. Actually, there is a third alternative, of following the skyline round in an arc over Sergeant Man, but personally I don't think the detour is interesting enough to justify the extra expenditure of energy.

Pavey Ark 2288ft Descend on steep cairned path

When you have dropped down from Pavey Ark, cross the stream, head generally west across the lower slopes of Blea Rigg, and you'll find an easy, cairned path which gains the top of the wide ridge behind Castle Howe without much of an ascent.

Cross stream and contour slopes to path

Cairned path

The good news is that it's either level or downhill from here. The bad news is that, again, this last stretch will probably take longer than you expect. As the path wanders among hollows and hillocks every pimple in front looks as though it will be Silver Howe, but another candidate beckons ahead when you get there.

Pass a small tarn, below you on the right, and fork right after a marshy pool, round the shoulder of the hillside. You'll probably find yourself at a very large cairn, just above the lower, flatter end of the ridge. Descend the path and follow it as far as a short rise, where you meet a transverse path. Turn right, and this path angles down along the

Large cairn

Right at smaller cairn

southern side of the ridge. At the second down-ward-plunging cross path, turn right again, and you will reach the road very close to the free car park.

It does seem at least eighteen miles, doesn't it?

WASDALE SUMMITS

A superb mountain day

15mls/24km   12 hrs
Ascent: 7,800ft/2,375m

Scafell – Scafell Pike – Great Gable – Kirkfell – Pillar – Scoatfell – Red Pike – Yewbarrow. Some of the best-known summits in the Lake District. You will collect them all in the course of a day's walk round the head of England's most dramatic mountain valley.

OS Outdoor Leisure Map South West Lakes or Harveys Western Lakeland

The distance is modest, the height gained considerable. I scanned the map with a magnifying glass, and jotted down a long list of numbers. Eventually, I decided to rely on the official figures for the famous Wasdale Fell Race, which follows a similar line round the dale head. The runners' ascent of Illgill, above the screes, is almost balanced by our inclusion of Kirkfell and Scafell. In case you were thinking of entering, I had better warn you that the winners usually complete the twenty-one mile course in under four hours.

The starting point could not be more convenient: the National Trust camp site and car park at the head of Wastwater. Walk along the shore of the lake to where a footpath cuts off on the right to join the main path rising from the parking area below Bowderdale, the home of Jos Naylor, probably the most widely known of English fell runners. I believe he started running up hills to strengthen his back after an operation on his spine.

Start at GR 183076 Car park, camp site

1km on road

The path points up directly to the arrowhead crag that marks the southern end of Yewbarrow. Just when you are starting to breathe a little heavily, the path turns left over a stile and climbs more sensibly across the western slopes of the hill. Scrabble up a scree on the right and you will pop on to the ridge at a narrow neck. Turn left up easy rocks and you're soon on flat grass, with your first views of the steep crags encircling the head of Mosedale.

Yewbarrow 627m/2058ft

The descent of Stirrup Crag to Dore Head is steep, needing hands as well as feet on the upper half.In recompense, the ascent of Red Pike is a steady gradient that soon levels out on an easy path. At Scoatfell, the path swings round to the right, but if you have started early, spare a few minutes to go to the top of Steeple.

Red Pike 825m/ 2707ft
Scoatfell 842m/2760ft

When I went round the route to refresh my memory for the guide, I intended to make a fast circuit. But my ambitions faded as the day became hotter. I positively dawdled along this longest high level section of the route to Pillar, enjoying my elevated situation on a glorious day.

Pillar 892m/2927ft

Kirk Fell must be a contender for the title of high Lakeland peak least visited for its own sake. The top is a tilted plateau, and the summit is on the further side overlooking Wasdale. From Black Sail pass I found my way up a gully of red shale and headed straight across to the descent path. If you want to reduce the amount of ascent, Kirk Fell is the summit to sacrifice. Especially as a path below the northern cliffs takes you across easily to the next dip before Great Gable.

Kirk Fell 802m/2631ft

I dawdled so effectively that it took me all of six hours to top out on Gable, and I indulged myself

Great Gable 899m/2949ft

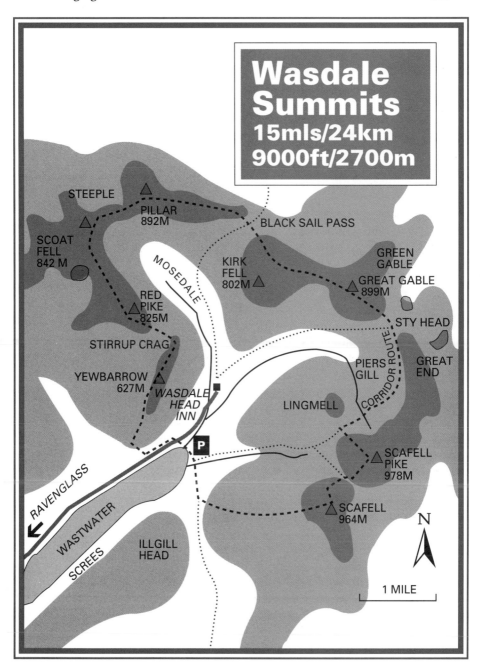

**Wasdale
Summits
15mls/24km
9000ft/2700m**

STEEPLE

PILLAR
892M

BLACK SAIL PASS

SCOAT
FELL
842 M

MOSEDALE

KIRK
FELL
802M

GREEN
GABLE

GREAT GABLE
899M

RED
PIKE
825M

STY HEAD

STIRRUP CRAG

PIERS
GILL

CORRIDOR ROUTE

GREAT
END

YEWBARROW
627M

WASDALE
HEAD
INN

LINGMELL

P

SCAFELL
PIKE
978M

RAVENGLASS

WASTWATER

SCREES

ILLGILL
HEAD

SCAFELL
964M

N

1 MILE

further by stretching out for half an hour to soak
up the sun and scenery. Perhaps I was reluctant
to slither down that long ribbon of scree which
masquerades as the path to Sty Head.

Whenever I cross over Sty Head I think that it
would be a perfect spot for one of those little
chalet restaurants you find on many alpine
passes. It would have to be discreetly placed of
course, perhaps with a terrace overlooking the
tarn where you could sit and sip a long cool drink
in the afternoon. There could only be one name
for the café: The Wainwright.

Whilst we're thinking continental, the path known
as the Corridor Route, which mounts across the
cliffs of Great End, does have the drama of an
alpine path, especially where it crosses Piers Gill.
You could be fooled into thinking it's going to
take a couple of hours to reach the saddle between Lingmell and Scafell Pike.

Corridor Route

It can be all downhill from here. If you choose to
go straight back to the camp site, you've still had
a superb mountain day. But it would be a pity to
miss out the highest summit in England, especially as the ascent from the saddle is one of the
easiest of the day. Even on tired legs it's only half
an hour.

Now you're on top you have to decide whether or
not you are going for broke by taking in Scafell. I
had thought of urging you to take the ridge
direct, up Broad Stand, but an overheard conver-
sation on the summit of. Scafell Pike, about a girl
who had fallen on the climb, confirmed my
doubts. And after all, there are many short scrambles in the Lakes, but only one Lord's Rake.

Scafell Pike
978m/3210ft

Wasdale

So if you haven't decided to call it a day, and slide straight down the screes from Mickledore gap, sidle under the walls of Scafell Crag. It's hard to believe that it's getting on for eighty years since serious routes such as Central Buttress were first climbed. They were brave leads for the time, with such primitive equipment and protection techniques.

Lord's Rake is, of course, the scree-filled cleft between the main crag and a semi-detached spear of rock. Nowadays there seems to be less scree and more bare earth, making it difficult for the soles to get a grip. It's an experience not to be missed.

Lord's Rake

Eventually, you step on to grass not far below the summit ridge. It's an undistinguished top point for such impressive cliffs. Don't follow the line of the ridge down, or you will find yourself descending unpleasant boulder slopes to Eskdale. Aim towards the head of Wastwater, roughly west. You are soon down on to steep grass slopes. Join the well-used path from Boot where it goes through a gate in the fell wall.

Scafell 964m/3162ft

That's it. All you have to do now is sit by the Wasdale Head Inn in the evening sunshine and follow your route again with your eyes.

NOT QUITE WAINWRIGHT

A North West Fells switchback

20miles/32km   9 hours

Ascent: 7,100ft/2,165m

In their search for new challenges, walkers and fell runners have gained inspiration from a variety of sources, literary as well as geographic. An example is the completion in one round of all the summits in a Wainwright guidebook. Personally, I prefer an elegant natural line to a route that follows artificial connections. But the two approaches almost coincide in this circuit of the north west fells.

Walkers who do attempt to bag all the twenty nine tops in the Wainwright guide usually need a whole twenty four hours. I believe the first successful completion of the circuit was by fell runner Chris Bland in 1983. On the sixth of seven consecutive days running all the Wainright-recorded Lakeland tops, he took only sixteen hours to cover almost 47 miles with 15,000 feet of ascent.

OS English Lakes North West or Harveys' North West Lakeland

Happily, you can climb most of the highest tops in the course of a more modest day if you keep south of the Whinlatter Pass. In essence, the route links up the Coledale Round with the Newlands Round. None of the hills is particularly high, but as soon as you are on top of one you have to swoop down again. I found the route tougher than I had expected. Perhaps I was off-colour that day. It was even a little hard to stay in front of a dog named Boss who was taking a girl for walk.

Start at Braithwaite GR 226237 Small car park at start of path More space on Braithwaite Common. Or get the bus from Keswick.

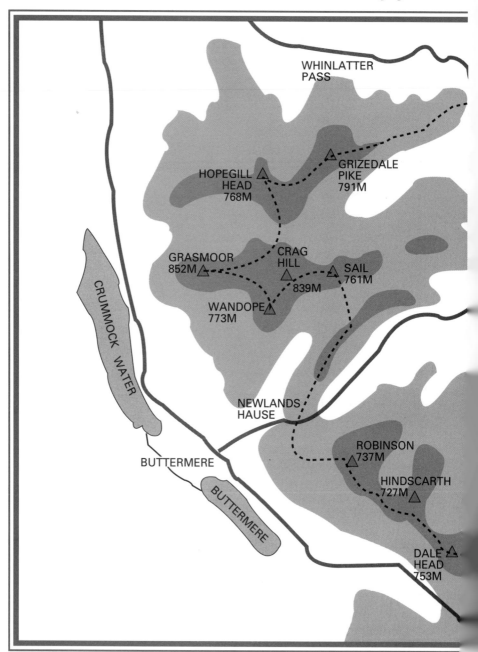

WHINLATTER
PASS

GRIZEDALE
PIKE
791M

HOPEGILL
HEAD
768M

CRAG
HILL

GRASMOOR
852M

SAIL
761M

839M

WANDOPE
773M

CRUMMOCK WATER

NEWLANDS
HAUSE

BUTTERMERE

ROBINSON
737M

BUTTERMERE

HINDSCARTH
727M

DALE
HEAD
753M

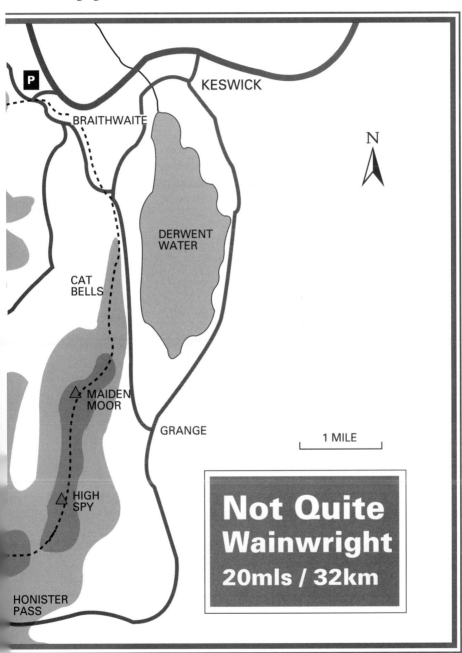

KESWICK

BRAITHWAITE

N

DERWENT
WATER

CAT
BELLS

MAIDEN
MOOR

GRANGE

1 MILE

HIGH
SPY

Not Quite
Wainwright
20mls / 32km

HONISTER
PASS

The relentless ascent of Grisedale Pike starts immediately from the car park above Braithwaite. A
line of steep steps curls up to the top of the first
rise. There, straight in front, is a hill walker's
pathway to paradise: a wide green trail bordered
by bracken, seemingly ending in the bright blue   *Climb Grisedale Pike*
sky. When you get to the vanishing point, the
metaphor develops rather less pleasantly. The
path continues to wind up the ridge, getting steeper as it nears the top of the Pike. It reminded me
of those Victorian engravings, where the righteous
few struggle up the stony path to heaven whilst
the doomed multitudes crowd along the easy
valley path that finishes in a drop to the firey
furnaces. Ah well, it was nice to be on the side of
the angels for a change.

From the top of Grisedale Pike, you get an im-   *Grisedale Pike/2593ft*
pression that the hills were waves of liquid rock   *791m*
which suddenly became solidified. Immediately in   *Hopegill Head/2525ft*
front, Hopegill Head was seemingly caught as it   *720m*
reared up from the south, its northern edge dropping sharply from the crest. You swoop down
from the Pike, then up again to the Head, almost
maintaining the momentum.

Then down again, skeltering on a shaley slope   *Coledale Hause*
that reminded me the studs on my shoes were
getting worn. The path heads directly from Coledale Hause to meet the main route to Grasmoor
beyond the skyline, but you can cut off the corner
by crossing the stream and climbing the north-   *Cross stream to*
east ridge of Grasmoor. I persuaded Boss to come   *north-east ridge of*
with me, but his friend was determined to stay on   *Grasmoor*
the straight and narrow path. Perhaps changing to   *Grasmoor/2791ft*
Pedigree Chum would improve my grrr factor.   *852m*

Anyway, here we are on top of Grasmoor, which   *Descend on main*
turns out to be exactly that, with the just-about   *path*

summit at the further end. It's the highest point of the day. Turn back almost in your tracks and take a slightly divergent line down the usual ascent path to a grassy bowl. The extra little top of Wandope is on your right, only ten minutes away, so you may as well take it *en passant*.

Wandope/2533ft 772m

Crag Hill 839m/2749ft

Up again, round the rim of a steep-sided valley to the top of Crag Hill. Or should it be Eel Crag? It's a popular luncheon viewpoint, and will probably come at a convenient time for your own food stop. Carry on down the narrow wave line of hill, up the aptly named Sail and down yet again to Sail Pass. It you were doing just the Coledale Round, it would be an easy hour back to Braithwaite now. Some other time, on a short winter day perhaps?

Sail/2500ft/773m

Sail Pass

Turn south-west at GR 204205

For you, now, the moment has arrived to make the connection to the hills on the eastern side of the Newlands Pass road. Appropriately, the link is a sort of geographical hyphen, a sharp little ridge isolated between the two groups of hills. It's awkward, but it can't be avoided.

From Sail Pass a path cuts down across the hillside towards Buttermere. At its nearest point to the hyphen ridge, drop down to the stream, cross a path coming over from Newlands, then cut diagonally up on to the top of the facing ridge. You might just as well get on top of the ridge early, and enjoy the easy walking, rather than try to contour for any distance. In a mile or so, the ridge drops down from Knott Rigg to Newlands Hause.

Descend path for 300m.
Left at small cairn
Ascend ridge. Follow top to road

The Newlands half of the route has a less complex arrangement of hills, rather like a trident with prongs of unequal length and summits placed

Cross road to steep path

neatly at the junctions. You are faced with a sharp
climb to get on to the ridge that forms the head of
the trident. It's up the path directly opposite   *Keep on left-hand*
when you reach the road, not along the wide   *edge of marsh*
track which goes across to Moss Force. On top of
the first step in the ascent, turn left along the edge
of Buttermere Moss and you will avoid the wet-
test parts, eventually meeting up with a path
coming in from the right that will take you to the
summit cairn on Robinson.

I was up here on a wild December night a few   *Night games*
years ago, descending from Robinson to Butter-
mere in the dark in a snow storm with three
fellow – but female – members of a mountaineer-
ing club. They looked after me very well,
although one of them did insist on ignoring the
cairn that marks the start of the descent path, and
going down on a direct bearing over miniature
cliffs to Buttermere Moss and the top of that
strange sledge-run path to the valley. I'm much   *Robinson*
too polite to argue with a lady.   *737m/2417ft*

On this latest occasion, it began to look as though
I would be finishing in the dark again. After a
mid-morning start, it was twenty to five when I
left Robinson, which meant I had only an hour
and three quarters of daylight left in which to
cover the remaining ten miles, most of which
were on the hill. If you bothered to read the
introduction to the guide, you will remember I
assumed you would have the sense to tackle these
long routes only on long summer days. Naturally
I don't take my own advice – I did the walk in   *Descend south-east*
late October.   *on ridge*
                                                    Ascend to
The descent from Robinson down the connecting   *Hindscarth/2385ft*
ridge takes you further still from Braithwaite. It's *727m*
fast going, and the following climb is soon dealt
with. Unfortunately, the summit of Hindscarth is

half a mile out along the central prong, but there's hardly any ascent involved. I have to admit that on that October evening I gave Hindscarth a miss and went straight on to Dale Head.

Dale Head/ 2473ft/753m

You turn the corner at Dale Head and at last head for home along the ridge which provides the long western skyline of Borrowdale. Memory played me false here. I had forgotten there was such a steep, slow drop to Dale Head Tarn, and I wrongly remembered the remaining four miles of hill over High Spy, Maiden Moor and Cat Bells as being all easily runnable. So by the time I did reach the rocky little hillock of Cat Bells it was half past six, nearer dark than dusk and positively black when I finally slithered down the sporting little descent to the road.

Descend stone staircase to tarn

Swing left over High Spy

Path along Maiden Moor and Cat Bells

I hope you will be strolling along this ridge in the early evening of a summer's day, and able to enjoy the classic view across Derwentwater. All I could see was the twinkling lights of Keswick.

Go down the lane opposite, signposted to Keswick. Almost immediately, on a bend, you will see a footpath sign with the same message. This takes you direct to the town through beautiful woodlands and round the top of Derwentwater. The slight inconvenience of going by bus to Braithwaite in the morning is amply rewarded by this relaxing end to the day.

Straight on along lane
Path on right to Keswick
Turn right in Portinscale over bridge

If you parked in Braithwaite, keep on the lane until you reach a signpost pointing left to Newlands Valley. Follow this lane to Swinside, and turn right at the pub to Braithwaite. I can't tell you much about this road section as I jogged along it by the light of a head torch. I was an hour late for the evening meal at Derwentwater hostel, but the ladies there – as delicious as their cooking

First left, first right
4km on lanes

– had saved food for me. It didn't stay on the
plate for long.

Next day, I walked the whole way round Der-   *The morning after*
wentwater, all of eight miles. After a frosty start
the sky stayed blue all day, and the autumn
colours were memorable. At the head of the lake,
I heard the sound of horns and hunters over by
Grange. A fox suddenly appeared from that direction, paused as it crossed the path in front, looked
at me, glanced over its shoulder as though saying
"silly lot of people" and unconcernedly trotted
towards the lake. When nearly back at my starting
point, I sat on a boulder by the lakeside, and
enjoyed the warmth of the sun on my face until
the orange disc disappeared behind the Cat Bells
skyline. I mention this just in case you have
gained the impression I judge walks only by
distance and the effort involved.

Cat Bells

ULLSWATER FORTY

The ultimate Lakeland horseshoe

40mls/64km   16 hrs

Ascent: 8,300ft/2,530m

There are only four routes in the Lake District in this guide. This is not because there are so few challenging walks, but rather because generations of walkers have explored just about all the conceivable lines, and written them up in shelves full of guidebooks. So there is no point in my including, say, the Ennerdale Horseshoe, even though it is one of the best challenging walks in the Lakes.

Daring to think in terms of longer distances gave me the idea of the complete circuit of Ullswater. I have never seen this in any guide, but after I worked on the route, I discovered a newly published coffee-table book which described the same basic route. You might find it interesting to read it and get someone else's impression of this long and immensely satisfying walk. I have to say that I think my version is more practical as it does bring you back to your starting point.

*"Walking Britain's Skyline",
Tony Greenbank*

If you like the idea of the walk, but find forty miles too daunting, make it a two-day expedition. The road crossing at the Kirkstone Pass, almost halfway, gives you the opportunity to stay at the old Kirkstone Pass Inn. If you're with someone special, there's even a four poster bed on offer. For cheaper accommodation, carry on down to Ambleside and gain the high ground again up the eastern arm of the Fairfield Horseshoe.

OS English Lakes North-East

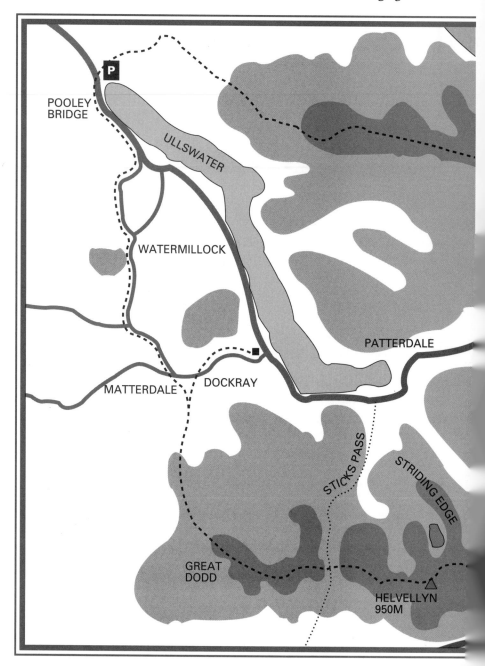

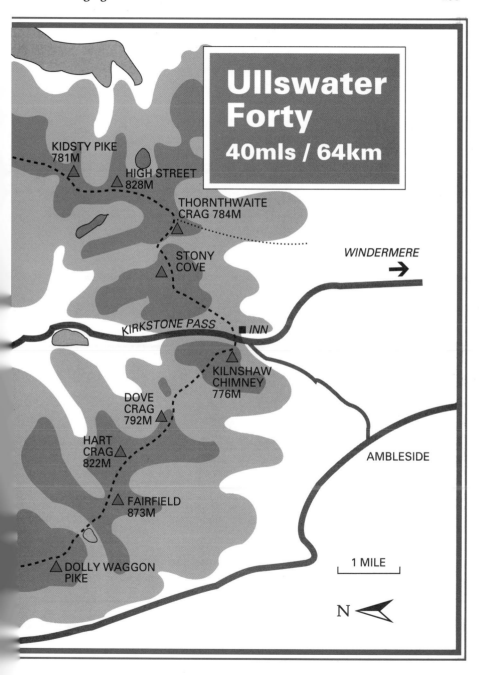

Ullswater Forty

40mls / 64km

KIDSTY PIKE
781M

HIGH STREET
828M

THORNTHWAITE
CRAG 784M

STONY
COVE

WINDERMERE

KIRKSTONE PASS ■ *INN*

KILNSHAW
CHIMNEY
776M

DOVE
CRAG
792M

HART
CRAG
822M

AMBLESIDE

FAIRFIELD
873M

DOLLY WAGGON
PIKE

1 MILE

N

Where else can you start but Pooley Bridge, at the very tip of Ullswater? Walk to the north edge of the village and turn right along a lane, across a minor road, and on to a bridleway. This climbs easily up on to flat moorland, where someone has helpfully placed a signpost indicating the line of the Roman High Street, both ways.

Start at Pooley Bridge GR 472244 Pay car park South-east on lane to moor

The problem is that the right-hand arm points between two paths which converge at the signpost. The first time I was up here, I dusted the cobwebs off my compass to settle the argument, but in the end adopted my usual approach of letting the landscape determine the line.

Right at High Street signpost

Is it heretical to suggest that many hill walkers nowadays are too concerned with trying to interpret a line on a map? Would they not find it more satisfying and possibly safer to look up and relate directly to the landscape? Whatever the way the legions went, it's preferable to trend towards the higher ground on the right. You get views both sides and it's drier underfoot. You'll probably keep just below Arthur's Pike. As you ascend an arm of Swarth Fell, the track becomes more distinct, and positively worn over Loadpot Hill and Wether Hill.

Navigation heresy - read the landscape

On your right now you're looking down the long trench of Martindale, with Ullswater glimpsed at the far end. On your left you can see Haweswater. In either direction, it's quite a long way to a road.

Head for the high ground and keep going

Up on High Raise and Ramsgill Head, the horizon is filled with the bulk of High Street mountain itself. You suddenly realise how high you have climbed on that seven or eight miles of moorland. The ridge narrows dramatically before merging with the whaleback of High Street. Look back for the best views of Kidsty Pike.

High Raise Ramsgill Head

High Street 828m/2718ft

The wide main track skirts the summit of High Street and continues at much the same level to Thornthwaite Crag, with its column-like cairn. The Roman Road keeps straight on to Troutbeck, but you need to turn right here, towards your first big descent of the day after ten miles aloft. The path curves round the drop at first, then plunges down shale to Threshthwaite Cove. Not surprisingly, you now have the first steepish climb of the day, up to Stony Cove. On a long route like this, I find it's preferable to rest on steep ascents. Pressing hard gains only a little time but expends a lot of energy.

Thornthwaite Crag 784m/2569ft Turn North-West and descend

Climb up Stony Cove

The trend is downhill now, over the tongue of hill that bends south above the Kirkstone Pass road. The path delivers you to the side of the Inn. You could treat yourself to a pub lunch here, but I would advise checking availability.

Kirkstone Pass. Food or bed?

If you stayed overnight, you will appreciate being fresh to tackle Red Screes and Kilnshaw Chimney. Presumably the latter name applies to a narrow gully near the top of the face. The climb is not as daunting as it looks. In fact, I think it's harder to come down the cliff. The path starts in a corner of the car park and goes round to the left, avoiding the steeper section of the crag. Tread delicately as you step up on the loose scree in the gullies – someone could be below. Last time I was there, I saw a young family sitting eating sandwiches in the direct line of fire.

Kilnshaw Chimney 776m/2541ft

In not much more than half an hour. you should be on top. The straightest route to the head of the short Scandale Pass descends over hummocky grass. Back on a well-used path, you wind up again past a tiny tarn to gain the Dove Crag ridge near a cairn that stands up on the skyline. From

Cross Scandale Pass

Dove Crag

here, you can follow the path that contours round
the hillside to join the route of the popular Fairfield Horseshoe, or cut up across the corner.
You'll probably find yourself with plenty of company on the steady ascent to Fairfield. Most of the
walkers will turn left on the wide domed summit,
down to Rydal Water. You go straight on down
the west ridge to Grisedale Hause and Tarn.

Hart Crag 822m/
2698ft

Fairfield 873m/2863ft

Keep left of the tarn to join the over-used ascent
path to Helvellyn. Most of the old zigzag path up
the first steep slope above the tarn has been
destroyed by the boots of people sliding straight
down. Now, there's an ugly scar of scree that will
test your legs and energy at a critical point in the
route if you are completing the circuit in one day.
Even so, I hope you won't miss out the top of
Dollywaggon Pike, but I'll let you follow the track
to Helvellyn summit after that.

Dollywaggon Pike

Well, this is it. The highest point of the route,
reached rather late in the day. I wish I could
promise you that it's all downhill from here. In
fact, this is the longest high level section, five
miles from the Pike in the south. Great Dod at the
northern end is only three hundred feet lower
than Helvellyn, but its grassy character fools you
into thinking it's much lower. Still, the worst is
over. The climbs in front are short and far from
steep.

Helvellyn 950m/3113ft

If there were hordes of people still on Helvellyn,
you will leave most of them behind as you head
north. A few walkers might accompany you over
Low Man and Raise (another one!) to complete a
circuit down into Glenridding. When you cross
the Sticks Pass and start to climb the first of the
three Dods you are likely to find yourself on your
own.

From Stybarrow Dod a grassy ridge stretches out in the form of an 'S'. The going is easy, even for tired legs. You're soon over Watson Dod and at Gread Dod. Unexpectedly, perhaps, it's a superb viewpoint, with the fells sweeping away on all sides. It really is all downhill now so you can spend a few minutes enjoying the panorama and finishing your food and drink.

Stybarrow Dod
Watson Dod
Great Dod
2807ft/851m

The most obvious path leads straight on, to Threlkeld, the route taken by people attempting the Bob Graham Round, seventy two miles in twenty four hours. They would still have Blencathra, Great Calva and Skiddaw to cross. Your way lies down the broad north east ridge. Further down it divides. Keep to the left. The flatter sections are very boggy, but if it's been a hot day your feet might enjoy a little water cooling. The path takes you gently to a bridge by a fir plantation and on to an unsurfaced road.

Descend north-east
to plantation

My feelings on reaching this point raised echoes in my mind. I realised later that I'd felt the same coming into harbour, particularly on one occasion, when I'd sailed in down the calm path of the setting sun after a day of boisterous winds and rearing seas. Such a long continuous journey on the hills is in the nature of a voyage, I suppose.

I promised you a route of forty miles, and that's the distance if you walk all the way back to Pooley Bridge. But you will be on the road for most of the time. A little forward planning will provide a pleasanter finish by the lakeside only three miles further on, at the Aira Force car park.

40 miles or 36?
Alternative finish Aira
Force car park
GR 401199

If you make prior contact with a taxi company, you can telephone from the car park. Even better, if you are doing the walk with friends, leave one

Call boxes at Aira
and Dockray

car at Aira Force. And this is one route where I suggest it is sensible to have a companion. The last hill section over the Dods and Matterdale Common will be very lonely late in the evening.

So from the bridge, follow the track alongside the plantation to a crossroads and on down into Dockray. Turn right down the hill to Aira Force car park.

If you are determined to walk all the way to Pooley Bridge turn left on to a path at a sharp bend half a mile short of Dockray. This takes you down past Matterdale to the A5091. Cross over to the lane opposite, go first right through Ulcat, right at the next T-junction and follow signs to Watermillock and along the lake to Pooley Bridge.

40 mile finish

I don't expect you would want to walk this long route very often. However, there is a shorter, all-mountain alternative which you could enjoy at most times of the year.

Shorter all-mountain alternative

It could be called the Patterdale Horseshoe, as it circles just the peaks beyond the head of Ullswater. You gain the full route at the ridge between Ramsgill Head and High Street, via the delightful path which scrambles up past Angle Tarn. This starts between the youth hostel and Patterdale village. You can carry on round as far as mood, fitness and weather allows. Ideally, top out on Helvellyn and descend to Patterdale over Striding Edge and into Grisedale. But you could also drop down earlier, from Fairfield, along St. Sunday Crag. I reckon the circuit including Helvellyn is around twenty miles – still a very satisfying day.

LLANGOLLEN LOLLIPOP

A little light relief

16mls/24km   6 hrs
Ascent: 2,400ft/730m

This last walk is neither long nor challenging. See it as a sweetie for bravely taking your medicine on the longer routes. But you have to promise to do them all first.

The Dee Valley is surely the prettiest gateway to Wales. Shapely hills rise up to border the river, squeeze together at Llangollen, then open out again for the ten miles to Corwen. But there's no need to rush on to Snowdonia to find a satisfying hill walk. The valley which opens up north of Llangollen has many delightful corners, and is bordered by a skyline that includes a spectacular limestone escarpment and a ruined castle.

OS Landranger Maps 116, 117

Llangollen itself is a charming little town bustling with visitors on fine weekends. The attractions are steam railway trips, whitewater canoeing on the Dee, Castell Dinas Bran on its hill, and of course the annual International Eisteddfod.

Start at Llangollen GR 415420 Car park Youth Hostel

From the car park in the centre of the town, cross the old stone bridge and climb a short slope to the Shropshire Union canal. This was one of Telford's little jobs. His aqueduct across the Dee at Pontcysyllte, four miles down stream, is well worth investigating if you have an hour to spare.

Turn west along the canal and follow it for two   *3km 500m along*
miles, past the motor museum, past the Chain   *canal*
Bridge hotel, to its beginning at the Horseshoe
Fall. You might have to share the towpath with a
horse pulling one of the tourist barges.

The Horseshoe Fall is, alas, not some great natural
feature but merely a semi-circular weir on the
Dee, where water is collected for the canal. But
the riverside meadow is still a pleasant spot for a
picnic, and the destination of those barges.

Follow the riverside path as it cuts across to   *Left on lane for 1km*
sleepy little Llantysilio church. Join the lane as it *to second lane on*
curves round with the river, then fork right up a   *right*
narrower lane. Where a footpath sign on the right *Path in 500m*
points sharply back, take instead the wide track
which parallels the lane. You gain the hillside
over a stile alongside a cottage.

The trail mounts along by a wood then climbs
more open slopes towards spoil heaps of an aban-   *Climb to skyline*
doned quarry. Bear left on the ridge and reach the
skyline by any one of several paths through the
heather.

I'm afraid you are in for a shock at the top. A
wide track has been bulldozed along the ridge,   *Beware trials*
and further churned up by the wheels of trials   *motorbikes*
motorcycles. Don't ask me how this happened.

Turn right along the track to a miniature summit,   *Descend past old*
from where you can look down on the Horseshoe   *quarry to café*
Pass road. Skip quickly down the slope to put the
motorbikes behind you. You're allowed to stop at
the café on top of the pass.

Cross the café car park and a narrow side lane to   *Cross to field gate*
a gate which gives access to a green trail. This

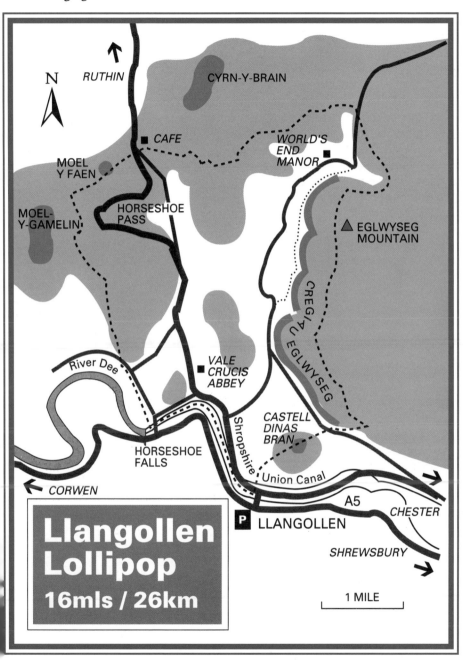

N

RUTHIN

CYRN-Y-BRAIN

CAFE

WORLD'S
END
MANOR

MOEL
Y FAEN

MOEL-
Y-GAMELIN

HORSESHOE
PASS

EGLWYSEG
MOUNTAIN

CREGIAU EGLWYSEG

River Dee

VALE
CRUCIS
ABBEY

CASTELL
DINAS
BRAN

Shropshire

HORSESHOE
FALLS

Union Canal

CORWEN

A5

CHESTER

**Llangollen
Lollipop
16mls / 26km**

P LLANGOLLEN

SHREWSBURY

1 MILE

trends gradually down across the hillside and
sinks into its own hollow before emerging by a   *Bryn-yr-Odyn*
small cottage at a lanehead.

The trail continues on the left-hand side of the
cottage, climbing up again by a fence, past a   *Lunch at GR 204478*
scoop in the hillside which makes an ideal lunch
spot, to a grassy ridge. You get a good view of the
Eglwyseg crags from here, great folds of limestone looking more like the Vercors in France than
Welsh border country.

The Eglwyseg escarpment

The obvious path heads down to the valley, but your route goes left, into a shallow hollow then round a shoulder of the hill. You join a water-logged track that takes you on to the lane which hairpins out of the valley.

4km from café

The valley head has the evocative name of World's End, and it certainly must have seemed very remote when the Elizabethan manor house was built there. If you have an interest in old houses, walk down the lane. Otherwise, cross the lane and follow a nature trail round the top of a plantation and back along the south side of a small gorge, to the start of the escarpment.

World's End manor house

GR 232477

You have a choice here. The skyline route goes off left to the upper tiers of rock. The second time you do the walk, follow instead the line of an unfortunately-positioned new fence along the lower rim, down a shelf path on to the Offa's Dyke Trail. It threads dramatically across screes directly under the cliffs.

Offa's Dyke Trail alternative

For now, though, the route stays on top of the escarpment. Keep high, on the top rim. Narrow trods take you through swathes of heather, and a couple of times you drop into dips between the folds of the cliffs. Towards the southern end, short cropped grass gives easier walking. When you reach a fence, follow it down gentle slopes to a lane poised above the valley.

5km along cliffs

Turn right along the lane to a point directly behind the sharp little hill crowned by the crumbling walls of Castell Dinas Bran. Go left over a cattle grid, right over a stile, and attack the steep climb to the ruins. The effort makes you realise that the castle would have been very hard to capture.

Turn right on lane. Left to castle

Only a few angles of stone wall remain of the 13th
century building. On its isolated cone, it com-
mands the Dee Valley. In terms of our route, it
puts a full stop on the question mark of hills
curving round from the top of the Horseshoe Pass.

A wide path zig zags down the western side, no
doubt graded for horses. At the foot of the hill,
the path joins a rough lane, crosses a meadow,
slips alongside a school, and deposits you back in
Llangollen. Take your choice of tea shops.

Enjoy the view

Castell Dinas Bran (photo: Graham Beech)

CLASSIC ROUTES IN THE NORTH WEST

My original intention was to gather together a number of new or less well-known challenging walks, as alternatives to the classic routes. After completing this work, I had second thoughts. Everyone reading the guide is not necessarily going to be an experienced long distance walker or fell runner, who has already done the famous routes. So I am including short descriptions of some of the classic routes, to make the guide more comprehensive.

Peak District:
Marsden to Edale - 25 miles

This was one of the first challenge walks to be devised, back in the early years of the century. The attentions of game keepers must have given added incentive to a fast crossing. As the walk is on moorland, the line is not sharply defined. The most straightforward route is to stay in the Wessenden valley up to the Holmfirth road. The crossing of Black Hill is famously gluey. Again, it's best to keep to the valley, past Laddow Rocks to Crowden, on the next section. Climb along the line of Wild-boarclough to Bleaklow Head, and thence to the summit of Snake Pass. The easiest route from here is to follow the Pennine Way to Ashop Head and up on to the Kinder edges, past the Downfall and across to Edale. A more direct route is to cross the dome of Featherbed Moss, drop down into Ashop Clough, and gain the Kinder plateau via the deep inlet east of Fairbrook Naze. It's very quick from here to the top of Grindsbrook.

Yorkshire:
Three Peaks - 23 miles

I believe we have two teachers from Giggleswick School, over a hundred years old, to thank for this route. It's the challenge walk that any rambler can attempt because of its moorland character and lack of navigational problems. Erosion has become so severe on some sections that the outdoor establishment discourages the walk. When a road gets worn, it is repaired. Why doesn't the same philosophy apply to footpaths? Having said this, there are far better long walks than the Three Peaks – the flat section which accounts for almost a third of the distance is unexciting and boggy – so do it once and move on.

The start is at Horton in Ribblesdale, of course. Book yourself out at the café if you want to record your time. Ascend Pen y Ghent via the lane by the church. After that long flat section, reach the valley road again just over a mile short of Ribblehead. Don't be tempted to take the eroded direct route from Winterscales Farm to the top of Whernside. The path which circles round to the north is pleasanter and enables you to traverse the whole Whernside ridge. The rest of the route over Ingleborough coincides with my One Way Ticket route in this guide, but you go straight on at Sulber to Horton.

Lake District:
Ennerdale Horseshoe – 21 miles

You're always conscious of the sea in this excursion round some of Lakeland's most entertaining summits, including Haystacks, the Gables and Pillar. To do the route justice, I would need half a dozen pages in the main section of the guide. So I'll just mention that it's usual to go round clockwise, and remind you that there are two possible routes up Pillar. This is definitely one of the best mountain days in England – and perhaps more enjoyable if you sort it out yourself.

Lake District:
Jos Naylor's Charity Challenge – 47 miles

This is a new route devised by Britain's best known fell runner. It stretches from Pooley Bridge to Greendale Bridge, near Jos Naylor's home in Wasdale. It is aimed particularly at older hill men and women. Time allowance are 24 hours for over-sixty-fives, 18 hours for over-sixties, and 12 hours for over-fifties. Fifty-year-olds might find their time a little tight, but it should be a doddle for fit over-sixties.

The first part of the route follows the line of the Ullswater Forty as far as Fairfield - that is, Barton Fell, Arthur Pike, Loadpot Hill, Wether Hill, Red Crag, Kidsty Pike, Ramsgill Head, High Street, Thornthwaite Crag, Stony Cove, Kirkstone Pass, Red Screes, Hart Crag - and then cuts across to Seat Sandal, Dunmail Raise, Steel Fell, High Raise, Rossett Pike, Great End, Great Gable, Kirkfell, Pillar, Scoat Fell, Steeple, Haycock, Seatallan, Middle Fell, finishing at GR 143056.

If you want to qualify for a certificate, you have to supply written confirmation from helpers, and raise at least £100 for charity. Make your claim to Jos Naylor MBE, Bowdendale, Wasdale, Seascale, Cumbria.

Lake District:
Bob Graham Round - 72 miles

Bob Graham was a Keswick guest house owner, who at one time lived in Barrow House, now Derwentwater youth hostel. He inaugurated the circuit of 42 peaks and 72 miles in 1932. If you want to join the Bob Graham Club you will need to complete the Round within 24 hours. But if you are not a fell runner there is nothing to stop you using the route as the basis for a more leisurely, but still demanding, three-day excursion.

Fell runners start at Keswick Moot Hall, and there are protagonists for both ways round. If they go anti-clockwise, they will cross Robinson, Hindscarth, Dale Head, Grey Knotts, Brandreth, Green Gable, Great Gable, Kirkfell, Pillar, Steeple, Red Pike, Yewbarrow, Scafell, Scafell Pike, Broad Crag, Ill Crag, Great End, Esk Pike, Bowfell, Rossett Pike, Pike o'Stickle, Harrison Stickle, Thunacar Knott, Sergeant Man, High Raise, Calf Crag, Steel Fell, Seat Sandal, Fairfield, Dollywaggon Pike, Nethermost Pike, Helvellyn, Lower Man, Whiteside, Raise, Stybarrow Dod, Watson Dod, Great Dod, Clough Head, Blencathra, Great Calva and Skiddaw.

I suggest that the best stop-over points for a three-day walk are Keswick, Wasdale and Grasmere, all of which have accommodation. Only slight deviations from the fell runners' route are necessary. From Keswick, as you aren't in quite so much of a hurry as the runners, you can use woodland paths for most of the way into the Newlands valley. When you descend to Wasdale, you will have to walk the length of the lake if you are staying at the youth hostel, but there is a campsite and bunkhouse at the head of the lake. As Grasmere, you can follow the Round to Steel Fell, and walk down its flank to Thorney How hostel. Or you can cut off the corners via Easedale and Grisedale Tarn.

Try the Bob Graham Round on a summer Bank Holiday. You might be inspired to try for a 24 hour circuit.

ORGANISED CHALLENGE WALKS

If you are not an experienced long distance walker, entering an organised event could give you the confidence to tackle some of the more demanding routes in this guide. The following is a selection of challenge walks normally held annually in the area covered by the guide.

January

Two Crosses Circuit, Lancashire, 25 miles

That's Lyth, Cumbria, 25 miles

February

Anglezarke Amble, Lancashire, 21 miles

South Shropshire Circular, 25 miles

April

Mid-Wales Mountain Marathon, 20 miles

Duddon Landscape, 23 miles

May

Round Kinder, 25 miles

Spring in Lakeland, 29 miles

Pendle Marathon, 26 miles

June

Leek Moors Marathon, 30 miles

Ironbridge Challenge, Shropshire, 26 miles

Silvarn Round, Cumbria, 25 miles

July

Windermere Festival Walk, 25 miles

August

Limestone Limp, Ingleton, 38 miles

September

Open to Offas, Clwyd Hills, 28 miles

Bullock Smithy Hike, Peak District, 56 miles

October

Three Shires Challenge, Peak District, 26 miles

Long Mynd Hike, 50 miles

Entry details of these and many other challenge walks are given in Strider, the magazine of the Long Distance Walkers Association. The Membership Secretary is Geoff Saunders, 117 Higher Lane, Rainford, St. Helens, Merseyside, WA11 8BQ. Send a stamped addressed envelope for information.

CHALLENGING WALKS DIARY

Vale Royal Round: 36 miles

DATE   TIME TAKEN

COMMENTS

Tops & Bottoms - Western Peak: 25 miles

DATE   TIME TAKEN

COMMENTS

Derwentdale Watershed: 28 miles

· DATE   TIME TAKEN

COMMENTS

Kinder Runaround: 24 miles

DATE   TIME TAKEN

COMMENTS

West of Wenlock: 25 miles

DATE   TIME TAKEN

COMMENTS

Mary Webb Country, Long Mynd: 24 miles

DATE   TIME TAKEN

COMMENTS

Clwyd Crests: 22$^1/_2$ miles or 30 miles

DATE   TIME TAKEN

COMMENTS

Berwyn Challenge: 30 miles

DATE   TIME TAKEN

COMMENTS

Betws Lakes & Forest: 17 miles or 20 miles

DATE   TIME TAKEN

COMMENTS

Carnedd Collection 22 miles or 30 miles

DATE   TIME TAKEN

COMMENTS

Welsh 3,000ft Peaks: 30 miles

DATE   TIME TAKEN

COMMENTS

Cnicht Connection: 20 miles

DATE   TIME TAKEN

COMMENTS

Craigs of Cadair: 22 miles

DATE   TIME TAKEN

COMMENTS

Bowland Double: 30 miles

DATE   TIME TAKEN

COMMENTS

Gates of Eden: 27 miles

DATE   TIME TAKEN

COMMENTS

Settle - One Way Ticket: 25 miles

DATE   TIME TAKEN

COMMENTS

Langdale Horseshoe: 18 miles

DATE   TIME TAKEN

COMMENTS

Wasdale Summits: 15 miles

DATE   TIME TAKEN

COMMENTS

North West Fells: 20 miles

DATE   TIME TAKEN

COMMENTS

Ullswater Forty: 40 miles

DATE   TIME TAKEN

COMMENTS

Llangollen Lollipop: 16 miles

DATE   TIME TAKEN

COMMENTS
